DISCARD

# HOLIDAY CRAFT AND FUN

Books by Joseph Leeming

FUN WITH WIRE
FUN WITH PAPER
PAPERCRAFT
FUN WITH PENCIL AND PAPER
FUN WITH BEADS
FUN WITH FABRICS
FUN WITH MAGIC
MORE FUN WITH MAGIC
FUN WITH PUZZLES
FUN WITH CLAY
FUN WITH WOOD
FUN WITH LEATHER
FUN WITH STRING
FUN WITH BOXES
FUN FOR YOUNG COLLECTORS
HOLIDAY CRAFT AND FUN
THE COSTUME BOOK FOR PARTIES AND PLAYS
FUN WITH SHELLS
FUN WITH ARTIFICIAL FLOWERS
FUN WITH GREETING CARDS

HOLIDAY CRAFT AND FUN

Party-craft for Holidays, including Invitations, Favors, Decorations and Centerpieces, Party Hats, Costumes and Games, Easily made at Home.

BY JOSEPH LEEMING
ILLUSTRATED BY JESSIE ROBINSON

J. B. LIPPINCOTT COMPANY
Philadelphia and New York

COPYRIGHT, 1950, BY JOSEPH LEEMING

PRINTED IN THE UNITED STATES OF AMERICA

TENTH PRINTING

Library of Congress Catalog Card Number 50-14621

CONTENTS

	page
GENERAL INSTRUCTIONS	11

CHRISTMAS *(December 25)*

Christmas Angels	13
A Paper Christmas Tree	14
Place-card Trees	15
Stained-glass-window Greeting Cards	16
Pine Cone Birds and Animals	16
Jointed Peanut Puppets	17
Walnut Shell Christmas Tree Decorations	18
Jiffy Tree Decorations	19
Yarn or Tissue Surprise Balls	19
Christmas Gift Wrappings	20
Shadow Portraits	20
Thank-you Cards	21

NEW YEAR'S DAY *(January 1)*

New Year Party Decorations	22
Snowman Centerpiece	23
New Year Place Cards	24
The String and Ice-cube Trick	24
Checker Calendar Pitch	25

LINCOLN'S BIRTHDAY *(February 12)*

Lincoln's Birthday Decorations	26
Drum Centerpiece	27
Red-White-and-Blue Hats	27
Lincoln Penny Place Cards	28
Tall Hat Favors	29
Penny Wise	29
Paper-plate Rolling Game	30

ST. VALENTINE'S DAY *(February 14)*

Valentines	31
Jigsaw Puzzle Invitations	32

CONTENTS

	page
Valentine Grab Bag Centerpiece	32
The Linked Hearts Puzzle	33
The Cinderella Dance	34
Pin-a-Heart-on-Me	34

WASHINGTON'S BIRTHDAY (February 22)
Washington's Birthday Decorations	35
Washington's Birthday Party Favors	36
Log and Hatchet Centerpiece	36
Crossing the Ice	37

ST. PATRICK'S DAY (March 17)
St. Patrick's Day Party Invitations	38
St. Patrick's Day Decorations	39
Paper Cup Party Hats	40
Cork People Place-card Holders	40
Peanut Pushing Race	41
Cardboard Bazoomer or Humbuzzer	41
A Comb Kazoo	42
Tin-can Tom-tom	42
A Shoe-box Harp	42
Tin-can Cymbals	43
Cardboard Bean Rattles (Maracas)	43

EASTER *
Peep-show Easter Cards	44
Yarn Chicken Place Cards	45
Centerpiece with Easter Egg Candles	46
Decorated Easter Eggs	47
Changing an Egg to Confetti	47

APRIL FOOL'S DAY (April 1)
Nonsense Invitations	48
Clown Decorations	49
Clown Centerpiece	49

(* Easter is the first Sunday after the full moon which happens upon or next after March 21. It never comes before March 22 or after April 25.)

CONTENTS

	page
Merry-go-round Centerpiece	49
Paper Clown Hats	50
Straw-sipping Place Cards	51
The Endless Thread	52
Cardboard Popeyes	52
Magic Menagerie	53
Paper Cup Racing Planes	53

ARBOR DAY (Date appointed by each State)
Blotter and Seed Experiment	54
A Potato Porcupine	55
Eggshell Flower Pots	56
Sweet Potato Indoor Garden	56
Bottle Gardens	56

MAY DAY (May 1)
Soda-straw May Baskets	58
Crepe-paper Sweet Peas	59
Nut-cup Party Baskets	60
May Pole Centerpiece	60
May Day Party Hats	61
Crayon Art Class	62

MOTHER'S DAY (Second Sunday in May)
A Paper Carnation	64
Butterfly Flower Holder	65
Cardboard Flower Girl	65

FLAG DAY (June 14)
Flag Day Decorations	66
How to Cut a Five-pointed Star	67
Party Hats: Betsy Ross Cap, Colonial Hats	67
Unusual Button Place Cards	69
Crepe-paper Cutting Race	69

FATHER'S DAY (Third Sunday in June)
String Holder	70
Crepe-paper Coasters and Mats	71

CONTENTS

page

THE FOURTH OF JULY
- Paper Firecrackers 72
- A Potato Popgun 73
- Clothespin Gliders 73
- Crepe-paper Swirlers 74
- How to Make a Paper Cup 75
- The Alphabet Game 75

COLUMBUS DAY (October 12)
- Columbus Day Decorations 77
- Columbus Day Party Hats 77
- Walnut Shell Boat Place Cards 78
- How to Stand an Egg on End 79
- Potato Puppets 79
- Clothespin Fish 80

HALLOWEEN (October 31)
- Halloween Decorations 81
- Halloween Invitations 82
- Lollipop Witch Favors 82
- Pumpkin Centerpiece 83
- Halloween Costumes 84
- Paper-bag Masks 85
- Paper-plate Masks 86
- The Mischievous Ghosts 86
- Halloween Ticktack 87
- Paper-and-Pencil Mind Reading 87
- Walnut Shell Fortune Telling 88
- Wind-paddle Moaners 89

THANKSGIVING DAY (Last Thursday in November)
- A Walnut Shell Turkey 90
- Clothespin People 91
- Wishbone Skipjacks 92
- Changing an Orange into an Apple 92
- Feeding the Elephant 93

HOLIDAY CRAFT AND FUN

GENERAL INSTRUCTIONS

PARTY CRAFT

This is a party craft book for boys and girls and older party-givers, too, who enjoy making things and sharing them with their friends. Making party decorations, gadgets and games is fun. With a little time and effort you can make beautiful decorations and amusing novelties that will surprise and delight your guests. All the decorations, favors, games and gadgets suggested in the following pages are simple to make and are of materials easy to obtain. Many of these home party ideas can be used in school or camp too.

TOOLS AND MATERIALS

It is a good idea to have a party box or kit in which to keep all the tools and materials you need for party craft. A sturdy cardboard box about the size of a large dress box will do nicely. In it you should have: a pair of sharp shears, ruler, tape measure, spool wire, needles and thread, staple fastener, gummed tape, library paste, glue, tacks, thumbtacks and string.

You might use another large box to store folds of crepe paper, shirt cardboards, ribbons, corks, walnut shells, pine cones, nut cups, paper cups and dowel sticks. Try to store large sheets of paper and cardboard where they will not be bent or torn.

Most of the decorations, favors and games described here are made of construction paper, mat stock, bristol board, crepe paper, cardboard and boxes. They are all easy to obtain.

Construction paper is inexpensive colored paper about the weight of drawing paper. It is sold in packages 9 x 12 inches and 12 x 18 inches. Most ten cent stores carry it.

Mat stock is heavier than construction paper. It has a dull surface and is made in beautiful colors. It comes in large sheets and is very good for posters and large cutouts.

Bristol board is heavy paper that also comes in large sheets. It is made is several weights, grades and colors. It can be had with either dull or shiny surface. Mat stock and bristol board are sold in art supply shops. Your local printer too may sell you some.

Crepe paper is an excellent inexpensive material to use. The grain of crepe paper runs the width of the fold. Cutting across the grain is cutting along the length of the paper.

Crepe-paper streamers: To cut paper streamers easily, slip the crepe paper partly from the package, measure two inches, and run two or three pins through the wrappings and the crepe paper to keep it from slipping. Then using the wrapper as a guide, cut through the entire thickness of the fold with sharp shears.

Cutouts: To enlarge cutouts, mark off large sheets of wrapping paper into one-inch squares and copy the motifs from the diagrams. Cut out these patterns and use them as a guide to make your cutouts.

Choose colors in keeping with the theme of your party and keep to that color scheme. Work out a unit of decoration. This will give you a gauge for the amount of material you will need for the rest of the decorating. Remember that decorations are seen at a distance. Make them large and simple. Try to keep the principal decorations at eye level or a little above.

Remember, too, that your decorations are temporary. Plan them so that they are easy to put up and take down. Try not to use nails. Use small tacks only when necessary. You will find that wire, string, mending tape, thumbtacks and small screw eyes are all you need use.

CHRISTMAS

Christmas is the merriest holiday of the year and December days are busy with joyous preparation, whisperings and fun. There is so much to do, so many things to make, Christmas cards, decorations and gifts. Let's begin early, so we will have everything ready on time.

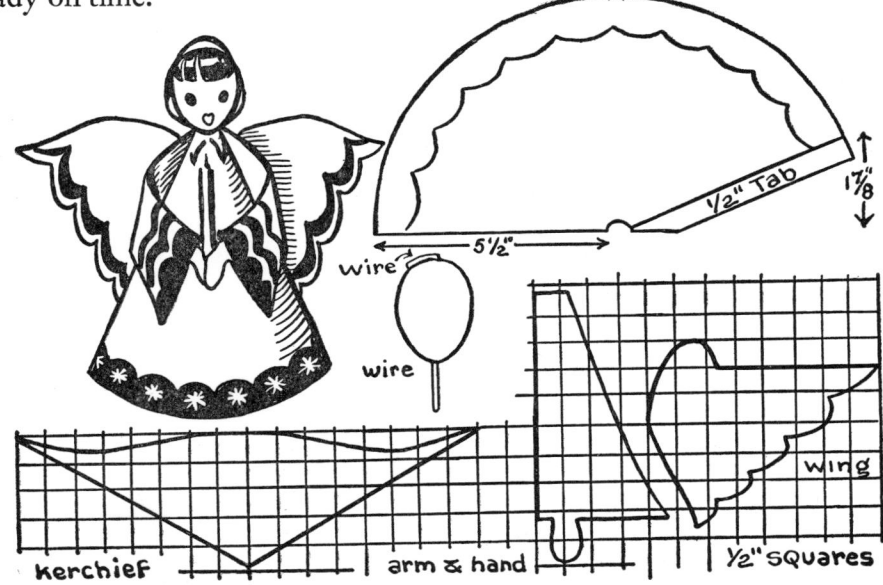

CHRISTMAS ANGELS

These Christmas angels with eggshell heads are good fun to make for Christmas decorations. They are very attractive when they are colored with paints.

Start by emptying an eggshell of the egg it contains. To do this, make a small hole in each end of the egg with a pin. Hold the egg over a bowl and blow hard on one end until all the egg is blown from the shell. The large end of the egg is the top of the head. Insert a piece of small copper wire about 3½ inches long through the hole in the bottom of the eggshell and up through the hole in the top so it extends above the top about ⅜ inch. Bend this end of the wire down against the shell and fasten it with a small piece of Scotch tape. At the bottom put a drop of glue around the hole where it touches the wire.

The drawings show how to make the angel's dress, arms, kerchief and wings. Make the dress and arms of white paper, and the wings of silver paper. Make the kerchief of blue or other colored paper.

Assemble the pieces, fastening them with glue. Then paint the eyes, nose and mouth with water colors or tempera paints. Glue on hair of brown or yellow yarn. Attach the head to the dress by inserting the wire of the head into the hole in the top of the dress. Fasten the wire to the inside of the front of the dress with scotch tape.

Bring the arms forward. Put glue on the inside of the hands. Then put a small 2-inch birthday candle between the hands and glue it in place.

These are for table decorations or they may be hung on the Christmas tree.

A PAPER CHRISTMAS TREE

This attractive Christmas tree is made by fitting a number of green or blue paper disks to a piece of wooden dowel set in a wood-block base. When it is completed and decorated with gummed paper stars or snowflakes cut from paper lace doilies, it makes a wonderful Christmas decoration.

You can use any number of disks, setting them closer together, if you wish, than on the tree shown in the drawing. The size of the bottom disk determines the spread of the branches, and each succeeding disk is cut to a smaller diameter. This makes the tree taper naturally.

Cut a wedge-shaped piece from each disk and paste the cut edges together. Scallop or serrate its bottom edges with a pair of scissors. Cut a hole at the center to permit the disk to be fitted to the dowel tree-trunk. Fasten the disks to the dowel with strips of gummed tape.

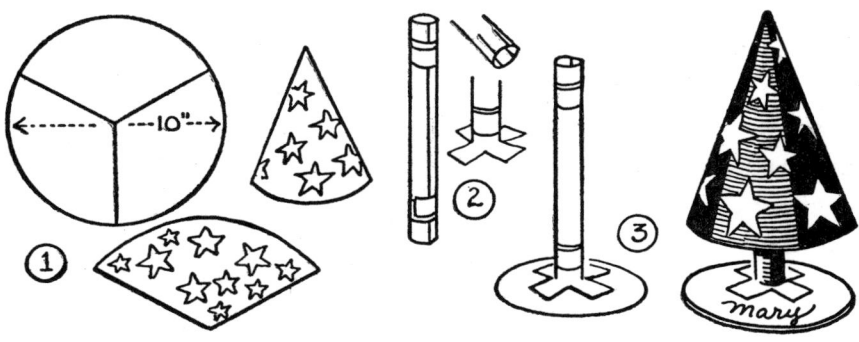

PLACE-CARD TREES

You can make little place-card trees of green construction paper and cardboard. Using a dinner plate as a guide, mark a circle on green, red or blue construction paper. (1) Cut out the circle and divide it into three parts. This makes three trees. Paste small silver stars all over the wedges. Paste the straight edges together to form a cone.

(2) Now, make a tube of brown or black paper, 5½ inches long, and 1 inch in diameter. Paste the edge or fasten it with paper tape. Snip into the bottom of the tube about ¾ of an inch, as shown in the diagram, and fold up the flaps.

(3) Mark a circle with a cup on cardboard. Cut out the disk and color it with tempera paint. Paste the tree trunk to this disk. Put a bit of paste on the top of the tube and slip the star-studded tree over it. Write your guest's name on the cardboard base.

STAINED-GLASS-WINDOW GREETING CARDS

Tissue-paper stained-glass windows are pictures or designs pretty enough to hang in your window. They make unusual Christmas cards. Parts of a picture are cut out, and tissue paper or cellophane of different colors is pasted behind the cutout parts. You can make some really wonderful effects.

Use thin cardboard for the base of the picture. Color it black with paint or ink. Draw the design or picture on the cardboard with pencil. It may be anything—holly, a Christmas angel, candles, a little village church or Old St. Nick himself. Look through magazines and books and you will find many pictures to use or copy.

When the picture is on the cardboard, decide what parts of it to cut out. Be sure to leave some uncut cardboard between the different parts. Cut out the parts you choose with a razor blade or sharp knife point. Then paste colored tissue paper in back of them. Draw eyes, windows and other details on the tissue with black or colored India ink. Write the greeting on the cardboard with white ink.

Punch two small holes at the top of the cardboard. Tie a string through the holes, so that whoever receives the picture may hang it from the window latch.

PINE CONE BIRDS AND ANIMALS

Pine cones can be used to make the bodies of many interesting, amusing or grotesque birds and animals for tree decorations. Thin legs may

CHRISTMAS

be made of wire, larger legs of matches or round applicator sticks that you can get at a drugstore. In most cases, you will have to whittle out the heads and some other parts from scraps of soft wood. Feet may be small pieces of wood, linoleum or cardboard.

Holes for legs or other extra pieces can be bored with any sharp pointed instrument—even an ice pick. In some cases you will have to cut away some of the pine cone's scales to make a place for the legs or to glue on a head. Attach the birds to the tree with string.

The drawings will give you enough suggestions to get started. Then you can devise other figures by yourself. Color adds a great deal. Use oil paints, and make the figures look as bright and lifelike as possible.

JOINTED PEANUT PUPPETS

Peanut puppets are amusing to make and are lovely tree decorations. Because of the different shapes of peanuts, they vary in appearance, and you can draw inked-on faces of many different kinds. Hair is made of yarn. Suspend the jointed puppets by a piece of black thread.

To start making a puppet, string four peanuts on a piece of strong thread, using a long needle that will go right through each peanut. The top one is the head, the middle one the body, and two lower ones form one of the legs.

Next make the arms. Run the needle and thread through a single peanut, drawing the thread through until the knot on the end rests firmly against the end of the peanut. Twist the thread twice around the puppet's neck, and then pass it through another peanut to form the second arm. Thread two other peanuts together for the second leg. Fasten it to the body by running the needle through the body, winding the thread a few times around the body, and then fastening it with a knot.

Make tissue paper or cloth clothes. You can dress the puppets as Chinese, Mexicans or any other way you wish, copying the clothes from pictures in books and magazines.

WALNUT SHELL CHRISTMAS TREE DECORATIONS

The walnut shell star and bird shown in the drawings are lovely Christmas tree decorations you may like to make.

Cut the star from stiff paper or light cardboard. Use colored construction paper if you have it; otherwise, color the star with paints or crayons. Paint the walnut shell with tempera colors or gold or silver paint. Glue the two halves of a walnut shell to the star, one on each side. Then punch a hole in one point of the star and tie a piece of string or narrow ribbon through it.

Make a paper pattern for the bird by following the diagram. Then cut the body and two wings from colored construction paper, or white paper which you can color. Make a small hole in the body and tie a piece of string through it. Paint the halves of a walnut shell gold or silver, and glue them to the body. Then glue the wings in place, as in the picture.

CHRISTMAS

JIFFY TREE DECORATIONS

There is no end to the variety of tree decorations you can make if you use a little imagination. Here are a few that are very easy to make.

(1) This Santa Claus is a paper cup with cut whiskers and crayoned face. His hat is a wedge of red construction paper pasted in a cone shape and trimmed with absorbent cotton. It is held in place by a loop of string threaded through the cup and hat with the knot inside the cup.

(2) Twelve colored drinking straws, each cut into three parts are bunched together and tied very tightly in the middle with string or fine wire to make this attractive pompon.

(3) Large spools and beads can be decorated with tempera paints to make attractive ornaments.

(4) This is a colored paper cornucopia with a frill of lace cut from a paper doily.

YARN OR TISSUE SURPRISE BALLS

Yarn surprise balls are always a welcome present for someone who is ill or to receive at his birthday or Christmas party. It is lots of fun to unwind them. The ball is made by winding yarn or narrow crepe-paper strips in which you wrap one, two, three or four small trinkets. You can use charms for charm bracelets and all kinds of *little* things such as you find in ten-cent stores and elsewhere.

Start by wrapping the yarn or crepe paper around one trinket. When it is covered, add another trinket, and so on, winding the yarn or paper until you have a good-sized ball. Keep the ball as perfect in shape as possible. Fasten the end with a gummed star or a bit of glue.

HOLIDAY CRAFT AND FUN

CHRISTMAS GIFT WRAPPINGS

Wrapping gifts in interesting ways is fun and adds to the attractiveness of your gift.

(1) Cover small food cartons with decorative paper or paste on cutouts, gummed stars or gummed tape.

(2) Red pom-poms and green braided yarn make this attractive package string.

(3) Use colored gummed tape and stars on tissue paper of a contrasting color for this package.

(4) Red crepe paper, green ribbon and thin cardboard make this interesting wrapping for a gift.

(5) This little container is cut out of colored construction paper, decorated with colored crayons and tied with a colored ribbon.

SHADOW PORTRAITS

On Christmas Eve or Christmas night, after all the packages have been opened and all the new toys tried, make some lifelike silhouettes of the family. All you need is black crayon, newspaper, a chair and a bridge lamp.

CHRISTMAS 21

Fasten a sheet of newspaper to a wall with gummed tape. Seat your subject sideways in front of the paper and place a lighted bridge lamp next to him. Turn off all the other lights in the room. Adjust the lamp so that a sharp shadow of your subject is cast on the paper. Draw the outline of the shadow with your black crayon. Then fill in between the lines. This is such fun everyone will want to try his hand at it.

It is fun, also, to make shadow figures on the wall by holding your hands and fingers in different positions to make the heads of animals and birds.

THANK-YOU CARDS

Be sure to add a little Christmas decoration to your thank-you notes to make them as gay as the holiday. Cut from colored paper or cloth a tree, a star or a sprig of holly and paste it on your card. If you prefer, use Christmas seals or decorate the card with colored crayon.

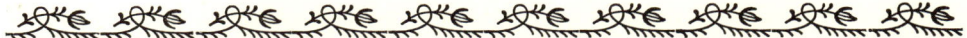

NEW YEAR'S DAY

NEW YEAR PARTY DECORATIONS

New Year parties are always exciting, but half the fun of the party is making the decorations and planning the entertainment. Think of all the things New Year's Day suggests: bells, icicles, snowflakes, snowmen. Use these for your decoration.

Cut out snowflakes and paste them to the windows with rubber cement. All you need is typewriter paper and a pair of scissors. Fold a 6-inch square of paper in half, then in thirds, and then in half again, as in the diagram. Folding the paper this way will make a six-pointed star. Cut and snip to your heart's content. No two snowflakes will be alike.

For icicles you need a few packages of white crepe paper—and some pale blue, too, if you wish. Cut a strip of crepe paper across the fold, the depth you want your icicles to be. Unfold the strip and refold it so that it will cut easily. Pin the layers together across the top edge. Cut the opposite edge in irregular points. Open out the icicles and thumb-tack them to the molding around the room.

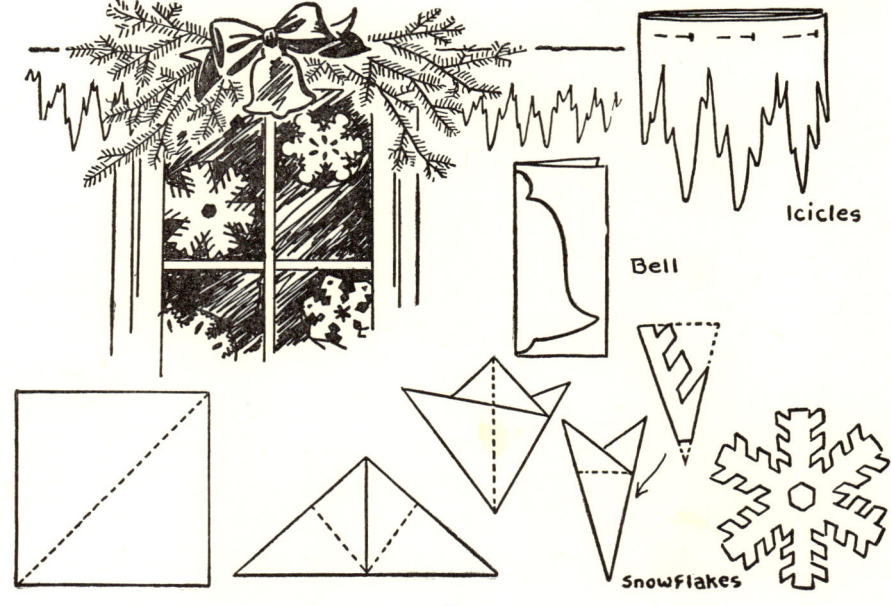

NEW YEAR'S DAY

SNOWMAN CENTERPIECE

This jolly snowman is made over a round cereal box or food carton. You will need newspapers, red and white crepe paper, absorbent cotton, a branch of evergreens and a few small bells.

To make the body, wrap crushed newspapers around the carton until it is almost round. Wrap 4-inch strips of white crepe paper (cut across the grain) over the newspapers to cover them and keep them in place. Then wrap a thin layer of absorbent cotton over the crepe paper and sew the edges together.

The head is a small ball of newspapers covered with crepe paper strips and absorbent cotton like the body. The nose is a little ball of red crepe paper pasted on. The eyes and mouth are bits of colored paper. Paste or sew the head to the body.

Make the arms of crushed strips of newspaper covered with crepe paper and absorbent cotton. Use red crepe paper for the mittens and then pin the arms to the body.

Give your snowman an amusing little cone-shaped paper clown hat or a high hat. The high hat is made from a paper cup covered with black crepe paper. For the brim paste on a circle of black construction paper. Make some of these little hats for your guests, too. See page 29.

Tie a red crepe-paper bow around the snowman's neck. Stick a sprig of evergreen into his arms and attach a few bells to the branch. Place the snowman on a bed of evergreens or a ruffle of red crepe paper and he is ready to grace your New Year party table.

NEW YEAR PLACE CARDS

To make these effective place cards you need a sheet of bristol board or heavy white drawing paper, a pencil, water colors and a pair of scissors.

Cut out cards 3½ by 4½ inches. On each card draw two lines and three circles, as shown in the diagram. Draw the hat, eyes, nose, necktie and arms. Color the hat black; the eyes blue; the nose and the necktie red. Cut away A, cutting carefully around the head and hat. Cut along the outline of the body to the dotted line. Cut a slit in the arms for the sprig of greens. Fold back B on the dotted line.

THE STRING AND ICE-CUBE TRICK

You can puzzle all your friends with this good trick. Start by putting an ice cube in a glass of water. Then give one of your friends a piece of string and ask him if he can pick up the ice cube with it and lift it from the glass. When all have tried and failed, as they undoubtedly will, you can show them how.

Loop the string and put the looped end on the ice cube. Then shake some salt on the string and the ice. The salt will almost instantly freeze the string to the ice. Then raise the string and the ice will come along with it.

CHECKER CALENDAR PITCH

This is a game of skill that you can get ready in a minute. It is a new and interesting New Year game to play with your friends.

All you need is one page from a big calendar, the bigger the better. This is the playing board. Any number of people can play. Each person has three checkers. If two people play, one has red and the other black. If there are more players, make pencil marks on red checkers, so each person can know his own.

Put the calendar on the floor. Then, standing five or six feet away from it, the players one at a time toss their checkers at the calendar. The object is to have the checkers land on the highest numbers. If a checker lands on a line exactly between two numbers, the smaller number is scored. Each player tosses three checkers, totals his score, and has other turns as the players toss in rotation. The first player to score 75 or 100 is the winner.

LINCOLN'S BIRTHDAY

February is a month of celebrations and on the twelfth we celebrate Lincoln's birthday. Abraham Lincoln was born in a log cabin and was a rail-splitter of the frontier before he became President of the United States. During his presidency, the Civil War was fought and the slaves were freed. In Washington his lanky figure and tall hat were familiar and well-loved.

LINCOLN'S BIRTHDAY DECORATIONS

For a Lincoln's Birthday party all the decorations should be red, white and blue. Blue silhouettes of Lincoln, eagles, log cabins and tall hats pasted on white stars or shields are good motifs to use.

The best paper to use for the cutouts is colored or white mat stock. Make the cutouts by the method described on page 12 and combine them with red and white crepe-paper festoons and streamers.

LINCOLN'S BIRTHDAY

DRUM CENTERPIECE

For the centerpiece on the refreshment table, make a red, white and blue drum. You will need a 5-pint ice-cream carton or a large tin can, red and white construction paper or mat stock, red, white and blue crepe paper, about 3½ yards of white ribbon and 2 dowel sticks.

(1) Cover the sides of the carton with the red paper.

(2) Cut out a circle of white paper to fit the top of the carton. Paste it in place.

(3) Paste the white ribbon to the side of the carton in zigzag fashion as shown in the diagram. You need to paste the ribbon only near the top and bottom of the carton.

(4) Cut out two 1½-inch strips of white paper and paste them over the ribbon points at the top and bottom side edges of the carton.

(5) Cover the dowel sticks with strips of white crepe paper. Make two small balls of red crepe paper and tie one to each stick.

(6) Tie the drumsticks to the top of the drum with a ribbon of blue crepe paper. Top it with a big blue bow.

(7) Place the drum on a ruffle of blue crepe paper.

RED-WHITE-AND-BLUE HATS

Any of these party hats can be made in a few minutes. All are made from the same basic pattern. Make them of red, white or blue crepe paper and trim them with the other colors.

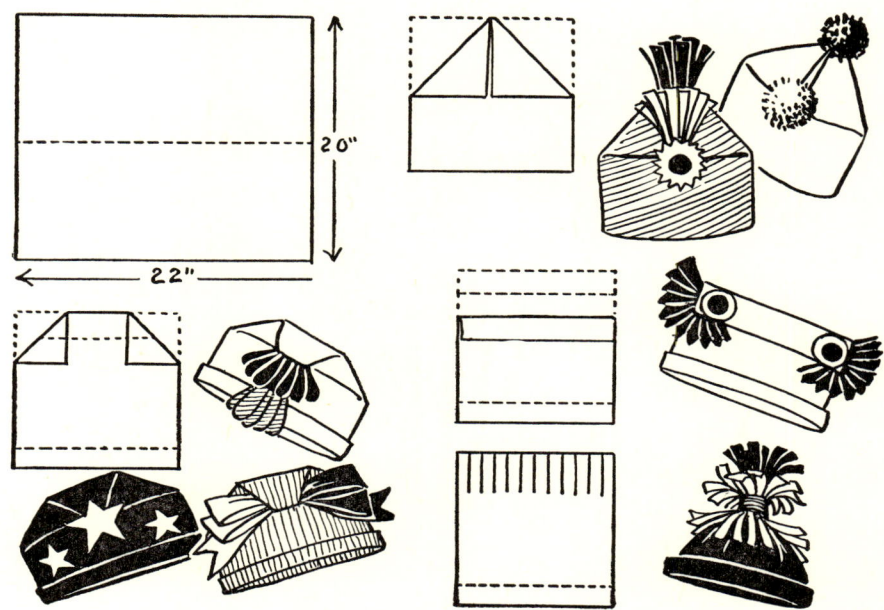

Cut a strip of crepe paper the full width of the fold of paper (20 inches) and 22 inches long. Fold the strip to make it 10 inches wide. The folded edge is the bottom of the hat. Stitch the seam up the back. Fold or cut the top of the hats in the various ways shown in the diagram. Decorate the hats with stars, fringes, pompons, cockades, or in any way you wish. Other variations will occur to you as you work.

LINCOLN PENNY PLACE CARDS

Lincoln penny place cards are amusing novelties and very easy to make. You will need a sheet of heavy white bristol board. (If that is not obtainable, use a piece of cardboard such as the laundry puts in a

LINCOLN'S BIRTHDAY

shirt.) You will need also crayons or show-card colors, and a shining new penny for each place card.

Cut out cards of the bristol board 3½ inches by 5 inches. Draw or paint a red, white and blue flower or figure on the card. Paste the penny in place for the face. Then turn back 1½ inches at the bottom of the card to make a stand, and write the names of your guests on the cards.

TALL HAT FAVORS

For these favors all you need are 4-ounce white paper cups, blue construction paper, narrow red gummed tape, paste, scissors and a package of small silver stars.

(1) Decorate the cup with strips of red tape.

(2) Cut out a circle of blue construction paper 4 inches in diameter. Paste the closed end of the cup to the center of the circle. This circle is the brim. Turn it up on both sides.

(3) Cut a strip of blue construction paper 1 inch by 7 inches. Decorate this with silver stars and paste it to the base of the cup to make the hatband. Then fill the cup with candy sticks.

PENNY WISE

Give each guest a Lincoln penny, a piece of paper and a pencil. Or better still, give each guest a sheet of paper on which you have typed or written clearly the following nine items—but not the answers. Then ask them if they can find the following nine things on the penny. They must write the answers within a given time, say fifteen minutes.

1. The name of a song (America)
2. A privilege (Liberty)
3. A part of Indian corn (Ear)
4. Something denoting self (Eye—I)
5. A foreign fruit (Date)
6. A perfume (Scent—cent)
7. A Chinese beverage (Tea—T)
8. Part of a plant (Leaf)
9. A method of voting (Ayes and noes—eyes and nose)

The person who has the greatest number of correct answers is the winner.

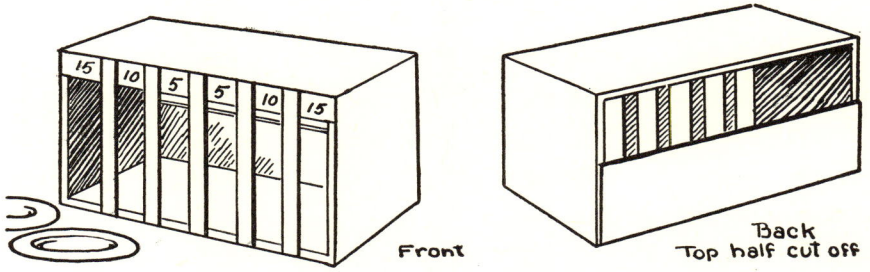

PAPER-PLATE ROLLING GAME

This is a good Lincoln's Birthday party game, at which, with practice, you can acquire a high degree of skill. It consists of rolling paper plates at a box with narrow openings in the front. Good aim is needed to shoot the plates into the openings.

Make the target box from a wooden apple or orange crate. You should be able to get one of these from a grocery store. Remove the top and fasten across it a number of cardboard or wooden strips. You can easily fasten cardboard strips with thumbtacks.

Write the numbers 5, 10, 15 and so forth on small pieces of cardboard and glue these above the different openings. These numbers give the points earned for successful shots.

Now remove one-half of the bottom of the box, so you can reach in and remove the plates after they have been rolled into the box.

Make a taw line either 10 or 15 feet from the box. Players stand at the line and roll three plates at each turn. The first player to score 150 is the winner.

ST. VALENTINE'S DAY

VALENTINES

February 14 is St. Valentine's Day. It is fun to make valentines and send them to our friends on that day. Valentines can be sentimental, funny or mysterious and can be decorated with cupids, bows and arrows, flowers, birds or hearts. Here are a few simple valentines you can make. With a little imagination you can design charming ones of your own.

(1) Cut out a card of heavy white paper to fit the envelope you are going to use. Then cut a heart out of red construction paper and paste it to the card. Cut out a red paper handle and paste it above the heart. Paste cutout flowers or paint flowers on at the top of the basket. Write your message on the heart or on the card.

(2) Paste a small red paper heart to a small paper doily and write the message on the heart with white ink.

(3) Try to think of other amusing ways to use a heart as part of your design.

HOLIDAY CRAFT AND FUN

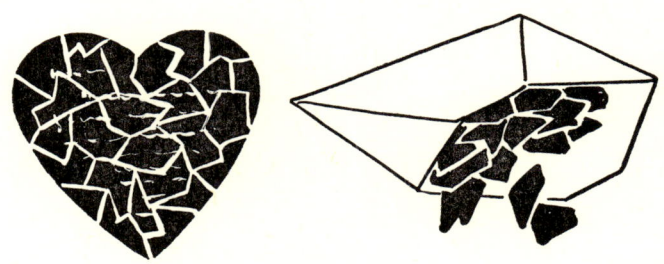

JIGSAW PUZZLE INVITATIONS

St. Valentine's Day is a perfect time for a party. Start your party fun with jigsaw puzzle invitations. Send your friends cut-up hearts that they must put together before they can read the invitations.

Cut out large hearts of red construction paper. Write your invitation on the paper hearts in white ink. (Most stationery stores have white ink). The invitation should read:

Dear _____,
   I'll be heartbroken if you don't come to my St. Valentine's Day Party on _____, February 14, at _____ o'clock at _____, etc.

When the ink is dry, cut each heart in pieces so that it looks like a jigsaw puzzle. Put the hearts into envelopes and mail them to your friends. To avoid confusion it is best to put the pieces of each heart into its envelope as soon as it is finished.

VALENTINE GRAB BAG CENTERPIECE

Grab bags are always fun. For this centerpiece you need a box about 8 inches square, 4 large paper doilies, red construction paper, white paint, paste and a yard and a half of narrow red ribbon or string for each prize.

Paste red paper around the outside of the box. Cut out 4 hearts of red construction paper and paint a heart face on each one. Paste the hearts to paper doilies and then paste the doilies to the box, one on each side.

Wrap and tie amusing little trinkets or puzzles such as the Linked

ST. VALENTINE'S DAY

Hearts Puzzle (see below) or a large jigsaw puzzle made in the same way as your invitations were made. Put these in the decorated box. Allow the long ribbons attached to each gift to trail over the box so that each person has a ribbon attached to his place card. One after the other your guests pull out their prizes, and the fun begins.

This grab bag is a variation of the Jack Horner pie. It may be used for other parties, too. To make a Jack Horner pie, simply fill a pie tin (or shallow bowl) with small wrapped gifts, then wrap the tin with gay paper or cover it with a decorated "pie crust."

THE LINKED HEARTS PUZZLE

This is a fine puzzle to baffle your friends at the table on St. Valentine's Day. It is not difficult to make from two pieces of fairly stiff wire. Bend the pieces to form two linked hearts, each about 3 inches high. The puzzle is to separate the hearts without untwisting the wires of which they are made.

Solution: Take the left-hand heart A in your left hand and slip the loop marked X through the center of heart B at the point marked Y. Then slip the loop X over the ring Z in the direction shown by the arrow. A little pull will then separate the hearts. To link them together again, reverse the movements.

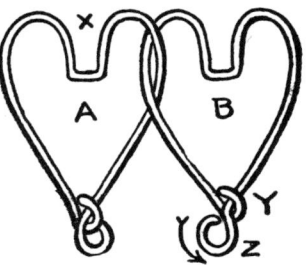

THE CINDERELLA DANCE

The Cinderella dance is an excellent "ice breaker" for a St. Valentine's Day party. It is lively and fun. The boys all go out of the room and the girls sit on chairs or benches around the room. Each girl takes off her right shoe and tucks her left foot (with the shoe on) under her so that it cannot be seen. The slippers are all collected in a carton. The box is then placed in the center of the floor and covered with a piece of cloth.

The boys come back into the room. Each boy reaches into the box under the cloth (without looking) and takes out a shoe. He then tries to find the owner of the shoe to be his partner for the next dance.

PIN-A-HEART-ON-ME

This is a variation of the old favorite, the donkey game. On a large piece of wrapping paper draw a figure like the one in the drawing. Give each player a numbered red paper heart with a pin stuck in it. The first player is blindfolded, spun around once and directed toward the figure. He must pin his heart where the heart should be. Each player follows in turn. The player whose heart is closest to the middle of the chest wins.

WASHINGTON'S BIRTHDAY

WASHINGTON'S BIRTHDAY DECORATIONS

Since George Washington was a very important person in American history we celebrate his birthday in every state of the Union with a holiday. Let's make our Washington's Birthday party gay with colonial hats, stars, flags, hatchets, and bright red cherries to remind us that Washington couldn't tell a lie when he chopped down the cherry tree.

Decorate the room with Washington cutouts, big red cherries and blue stars. Make patterns of the different parts of the Washington cutout. Then cut the various parts from colored mat stock and paste them in place on a sheet of heavy white paper. The face is pink; the wig white; the hat and coat blue; the ruff white; and the epaulets gold.

The stars are blue mat stock. Make a five-pointed star, 8 inches across, using the pattern on page 67. Then cut out as many stars as you need. String them on heavy thread.

The cherries are red balloons with green mat stock leaves. After the paper leaves are cut out, fold them down the center and then open them out again.

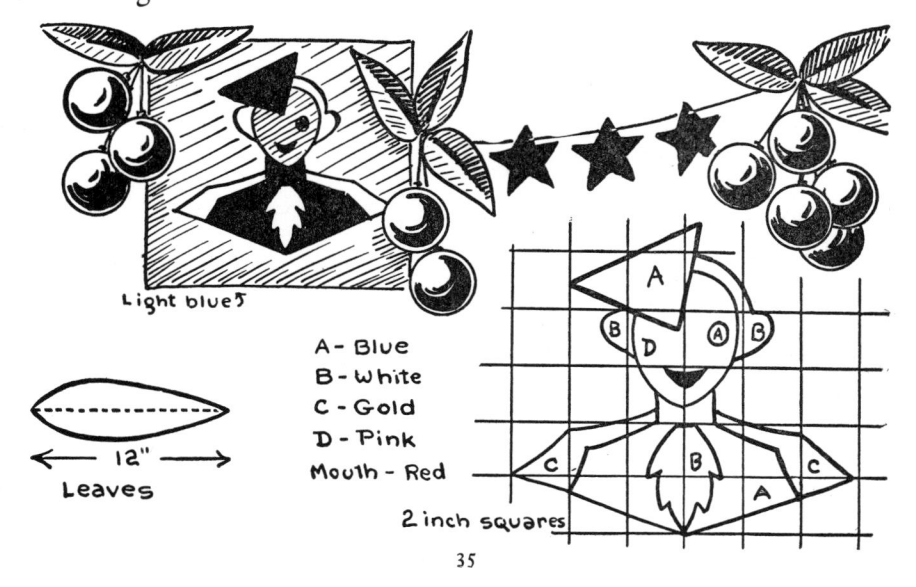

WASHINGTON'S BIRTHDAY PARTY FAVORS

For these little place card favors you will need some white paper nut cups, blue and red construction paper, paste, scissors and white ink.

Cut out a 4½ inch star pattern and make a blue star from it. Now cut out a little hatchet of red construction paper. Write your guest's name on the hatchet with white ink. Paste the hatchet to the nut cup and paste the nut cup to the star. Fill the cup with small candies.

Another easy nut cup favor is made by pasting a nut cup to a 4½ inch circle of blue construction paper. Fold up and paste the edge of the circle to the cup on three sides. Make a cockade of red and white crepe paper and paste it to the brim with a little silver paper star. These silver stars can be bought by the package in the ten-cent store.

To add color to your Washington's Birthday party, make colonial hats and Betsy Ross caps, see page 67, or red, white and blue hats, page 27.

LOG AND HATCHET CENTERPIECE

A log and hatchet centerpiece is very effective and not at all difficult to make, though it takes a little time.

The log is a round cereal box covered with brown wrapping paper or brown crepe paper that has been crushed and pasted loosely to the sides of the box. Paint the ends yellow with tempera paints and add thin brown lines to make them look like the ends of logs.

Cut the hatchet out of heavy cardboard, paint it red, white and blue and let it dry before painting the other side in the same way. Then cover the blue handle with little silver paper stars.

The plate is a 12-inch oval of cardboard. Use a small oval platter as a guide. Trim the oval with 1½-inch ruffles of red, white and blue crepe paper by pasting the ruffles, overlapping, to the oval.

For cherries, use hard candy balls covered with red paper tied with thin wire, two cherries to a wire. Tie clusters of cherries together, adding green paper leaves.

Cut a slit in the log and insert the hatchet. Paste the log to the decorated oval plate. Then place clusters of cherries on each side.

CROSSING THE ICE

This is a race that reproduces much of the excitement of Eliza's running across the ice cakes in *Uncle Tom's Cabin*. It is a stunt you and your friends can use at any time, and it is also a good party game.

On the floor at one end of a room place four paper plates, two for each racer. The contestants stand behind the plates. At the word "Go," each racer picks up one of the plates and moves it forward. He then places one foot on the plate and, balancing himself on that foot, he picks up the second plate and moves it ahead of the first. Then he puts his free foot on the second plate and balances on that foot while he moves the first plate ahead of the second.

The contestants must travel the length of the room in this manner, one plate or "ice cake" at a time. They must not at any time lose their balance or touch the floor with any parts of their bodies, or they will be disqualified. The one who finishes first is, of course, the winner.

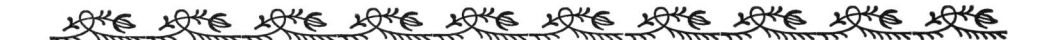

ST. PATRICK'S DAY

March winds may blow and it may snow but March 17 will be gay with St. Patrick's Day parades and parties. Emerald green flags, shamrocks, harps, pipes and quaint green hats will adorn shop windows and homes, for emerald green and shamrocks are symbolic of Ireland, the Emerald Isle. The harps are for St. Patrick and the pipes and green hats are reminders of the Irish country folk.

ST. PATRICK'S DAY PARTY INVITATIONS

PRINTING DESIGNS WITH POTATOES

Decorate your St. Patrick's Day party invitations with potato prints. You can carve out a design on a potato in a few minutes, and the printing is easy.

The drawing shows how the designs are made. Cut a potato in half. Draw the outline of a design on a small piece of paper. Cut it out and place it on the cut surface of the potato. Cut around the design with a pocket knife so it will be raised about half an inch above the rest of the potato, cutting out the inside parts of the design, also.

When the raised design is finished, brush it with ink or paint and press it evenly on a piece of paper. You can make rows of alternate designs by using two potatoes, each with a different design. Paper printed in this way can also be used for book covers, gift wrapping or to cover small boxes. A potato design will make good prints for only a day and then you must make a new design on a fresh potato.

ST. PATRICK'S DAY DECORATIONS

The drawing shows some interesting St. Patrick's Day decorations that are easy to make. The large cutouts are made of mat stock—the shamrocks are emerald green; the harps gold; the hats emerald green with white bands; and the pipes are white. For directions for making the cutouts, see page 12.

Pin or staple the cutouts to light green crepe-paper rosettes. To make the rosettes, cut a strip of crepe paper 20 inches wide and 30 inches long. Pull the edges gently to make them ruffle. Bunch the strip together in the middle and tie it with a bit of string or wire. Fan out the sides and pin or staple the overlapping edges.

This size medallion is good for a large room or gym. If the room you are using is small, make smaller medallions. Reduce all the dimensions by half. Mark your wrapping paper in ½-inch squares for the designs and make the rosettes from strips of crepe paper 10 inches wide and 15 inches long.

The shamrock festoons are made from long strips of green crepe paper. Stick a few pins into a package of emerald green crepe paper to keep the folds in place. Cut out a shamrock, cutting through all thicknesses at once. Be sure to leave a part of the leaf uncut on each side, so that when the strip is opened out, the leaves will be joined.

PAPER CUP PARTY HATS

Paper cup party hats are amusing and will add gaiety to your table.
Buy paper cups and crepe paper—emerald green for St. Patrick's Day. Cover each cup with the crepe paper, using paste. Then add a pompon, crepe-paper bow or other decoration. Pictures cut from magazines can be pasted to the front of the hat, or you can make cutouts from colored construction paper and paste them on.

To fasten the hat to your head, make a small hole at the rim of the cup, one on each side. Then pass a piece of string through the holes to tie under your chin.

Make a tall hat by pasting a circle of green construction paper to the bottom of the hat. Add a white paper band and a little cutout gold paper buckle. To tie the hat on your head, make two little holes through the brim and the cup, one on each side, and fasten a piece of string through them.

CORK PEOPLE PLACE-CARD HOLDERS

Save the corks that come into the house in various kinds of bottles or buy some at the hardware store and use them to make place-card holders for your St. Patrick's Day party. Use a large cork for the body of a human figure. Use a small cork for the head, and ink or paint on the features. Glue the head to the body. Legs and arms are made from hairpins. Twist the hairpin to make a single piece. Push the sharp ends into the cork body, and bend the closed end of each pin to form the feet and hands. Paint the cork bodies with green and white paint.

PEANUT PUSHING RACE

Peanut pushing is funniest when it is played at a party where there will be an audience to watch the contestants. Your St. Patrick's Day guests will enjoy this game, and you can paint the peanuts green, if you like.

Two to four people may race against each other. Make two lines on the floor, with string or tape, to mark the start and finish. Each contestant has a peanut and a wooden toothpick. At the word "Go" they are to push the peanuts across the floor with the toothpicks, each trying to be the first to cross the finish line.

If toothpicks are not available, you can use pencils instead.

CARDBOARD BAZOOMER OR HUMBUZZER

What is St. Patrick's Day without music? Make your own musical instruments and give one to each of your guests. The humbuzzer carries the tune and the rest of the instruments make the background noises. You'll make music to rival McNamara's band.

Some people call this musical instrument a bazoomer and some call it a humbuzzer. Both names give pretty good descriptions of the musical tones it produces.

It consists of a cardboard cylinder with holes in it. The cylinder may be a cardboard mailing-tube or a tube from the center of a roll of paper towels. It should be about 10 inches long and have about a 3-inch diameter, although the exact dimensions are not very important.

Punch a row of four or five small holes through one side of the tube arranged as on a fife. Then cover one end with a square of waxed paper held in place by string or a rubber band.

Now hum a tune into the open end and see what happens. The instrument will increase the sound volume to an amazing degree and give it a resonant, booming quality. By covering the holes with your fingers, you can produce different notes.

A COMB KAZOO

A comb kazoo makes quite an interesting noise. You make one by folding a piece of tissue paper or wax paper and putting it over a comb, as shown in the drawing. The teeth of the comb are against the fold of the paper.

Put your lips gently against the tissue-covered comb, being careful not to moisten the paper, and hum a tune. With a little practice you will be able to hum a song, or even accompany songs being played or sung on the radio.

TIN-CAN TOM-TOM

Tom-toms of different sizes and tones are easily made by stretching drumheads from old automobile tire inner tubes over the open ends of tin cans. Use small vegetable cans and, for bigger and better tom-toms, the larger cans used for fruits, fruit juices and jams.

Remove both ends with one of the twisting kind of can openers which turns down the edge of the can and makes a smooth rim that will not cut your fingers or the rubber. The drumheads are held in place by pieces of string wound around the can and tightly tied. You can play the tom-tom either with drumsticks or your fingers.

A SHOE-BOX HARP

A shoe-box harp is fun to make and fun to play. If you have the right sizes of rubber bands, you should be able to make a harp on which you can play a number of simple tunes such as "Jingle Bells," "America" and so on.

Make the harp by stretching rubber bands around a shoe box, as shown in the drawing. Use large and small bands and experiment with arranging them until you have a musical scale of eight or more notes.

The big bands make the low notes, and the smaller bands the higher notes.

You can play the harp by plucking the strings with your fingers. Also try playing it by rubbing an old toothbrush across the strings.

TIN-CAN CYMBALS

Cymbals for your homemade band or to keep time with radio music can be made from the tops of coffee tins or other food tins.

Get two tin-can tops and cut two wooden handles from 1-inch wooden dowels, from an old broom, or from any other wood you can find. With a nail, punch a small hole in the exact center of each cover. Then drive small nails through the holes and into the handles and the cymbals are all set and ready to go.

It is important not to nail the covers too tightly against the handles. Leave a small space between, and you will get a better vibration and a better tone.

CARDBOARD BEAN RATTLES

(Maracas)

You can have a wonderful time with a homemade bean rattle which makes a noise just like the maracas that you hear in Cuban and Mexican music. It will add rhythm to your home band.

The rattle consists of a cardboard tube such as a mailing tube or the tube that paper towels are rolled on. Cut two circles of heavy paper, each about 2 inches greater in diameter than the tube. Put one of these over one end of the tube and fasten it in place with glue and string.

Now put a handful of beans, rice and pebbles into the tube and cover the second end. Then shake the tube and it will make the soft rattling noise characteristic of the maraca.

If you wish, you may cover the tube with gift wrapping paper to give it a gay appearance.

EASTER

PEEP-SHOW EASTER CARDS

Easter is another time when it is nice to send greetings to our friends. Peep-show Easter cards are beautiful and unusual, and your friends will enjoy receiving them.

Cut a card from light colored construction paper. Eight inches wide and five inches high is a good size. Fold it in half as shown in the diagram. On the front half draw an egg. Paint the egg with bright colors. Cut around the outline leaving about an inch uncut on the left side, to make a flap. Open out the egg and draw the outline of the egg lightly on the inner sheet of the card. Inside this outline draw any surprise you wish, such as an Easter bunny, a baby chick or a little bouquet of flowers. Paste the corners of the two sheets together.

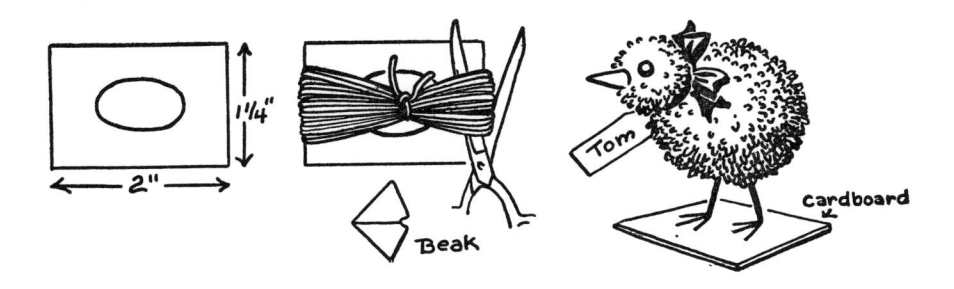

YARN CHICKEN PLACE CARDS

These little yellow chickens are fun to make at any time. They are most appropriate, of course, around Eastertime and make delightful Easter place cards.

To make a chicken, you will need a little cardboard loom, like the one shown in the drawing. It is simply a piece of stiff cardboard 2 inches long and 1¼ inches wide. Cut an oval hole, 1 inch long and five-eighths of an inch wide, in the center.

Yellow yarn is generally used for the chicks, but you can also use pink, blue or any other color you wish to. Wrap 40 turns of the yarn lengthwise around the cardboard, that is, from end to end of the loom. Cut off the remaining yarn and use a piece of it to tie all the strands on the loom together at the center. With scissors, cut the yarn at each end of the loom. You can then fluff out the strands of yarn to make a round fluffy ball. This is the body of the chicken.

Next make a smaller ball for the chicken's head. It is made in the same way as the body, but the yarn is wound around the loom from side to side instead of from end to end. Wind about 30 turns. Tie the strands together at the center and then cut them at the ends. Tie the head to the center of the body, using the free ends of the yarn that were tied around the center of the yarn after the head was wound.

Clip the yarn with scissors to make the head and body two distinct parts. Then glue on two beads or button eyes and a yellow paper beak. Add legs made of three pieces of wire twisted together. Spread out the lower ends of the wire to make the feet. Tie a little name card around the neck with colored ribbon.

CENTERPIECE WITH EASTER EGG CANDLES

Egg-shaped candles are easy to mold from bits of cold candles, paraffin and crayon stubs.

The mold for the candle is an eggshell. Punch a tiny hole in the pointed end of the egg, large enough for a piece of twine to pass through. Make a large hole at the large end of the egg. Shake the contents out, rinse the inside and let the shell dry. The membrane on the inside of the shell should be left intact.

After the shell is dry, thread a piece of twine for a wick through the small hole and out the large hole. Put the shell in an egg cup or small glass with the large hole up. Then prepare the wax by melting together candle stubs or odd bits of paraffin. Color the wax by melting in a piece of colored wax crayon.

Pour the liquid wax into the eggshell mold and let it cool. As the wax cools it will shrink and the shell will have to be refilled until the wax hardens flush with the top. Be sure to keep the wick straight. When the wax has set, remove the excess wax which may have run out over the shell. Complete the candles by cracking and peeling off the shell and trimming the wick. The candles may be decorated with oil paint to add to their attractiveness.

To form the centerpiece, set three or four egg candles on a dish in the center of the table. Place fresh green leaves around the dish.

DECORATED EASTER EGGS

Here is a new and amusing way to decorate eggs for Easter. It is a method by which you can transfer colored or black-and-white pictures from newspapers onto the surfaces of eggs.

The first step is to hardboil the eggs you are going to use. Then cut out the pictures you want to transfer. They must be small enough to fit on a part of the eggshell. Hold the egg in one hand and rub wax paraffin on the part where the picture is to go.

Then put the picture face down on the waxed part. Hold it there and rub its back with a spoon, as shown in the drawing. When you remove the paper, the picture will be printed on the egg.

There are many other ways of decorating and coloring eggs. You can use water colors, colored inks, crayons, the vegetable dyes mother uses to color frosting, or you can buy regular egg coloring dyes at the ten-cent store. These dyes come in beautiful colors, and are inexpensive.

Dip the hard boiled eggs in dye or paint them with imagination. Paint faces, flowers, dots, swirls, zigzag lines or initials.

CHANGING AN EGG TO CONFETTI

This is a very beautiful magic effect and a very surprising one to use at your Easter party. The magician shows the audience an egg, which he holds in his right hand. He closes his hand around the egg and waves it in the air. Suddenly a shower of confetti fills the air and falls to the ground. The egg has disappeared.

The trick is done with the aid of a "blown" egg. To prepare it, take an egg and make two small holes, one in each end. Then blow through one of the holes and the contents will be forced out through the opposite hole. One of the holes is then made a little larger and the egg is filled with confetti, which you can get at most ten-cent stores.

When doing the trick, hold your right thumb over one of the holes and your fingers over the other hole. Close your hand over the egg, and the gentle pressure will break the shell and release the confetti. The bits of eggshell will fall down, unnoticed, with the confetti.

APRIL FOOL'S DAY

NONSENSE INVITATIONS

April Fool's Day is the time for all kinds of harmless jokes and nonsense, a perfect day for a party. Start your April Fool's Day fun by sending your friends nonsense invitations that consist of two sheets of paper. On one sheet is written a jumble of words that doesn't seem to make sense. The other sheet has holes cut in it. On the bottom of this sheet write, "Place over the enclosed letter." When this is done, the invitation is easy to read.

You will need two sheets of paper for each invitation. Tear or cut holes in one sheet and place it over the second sheet. Write your invitation in the open spaces. Remove the top sheet and fill in the spaces between the words of the message with any silly words you can think of. This is fun—for your guests as well as for you.

APRIL FOOL'S DAY

CLOWN DECORATIONS

Clowns suggest fun, frolic and merry pranks. Use them in your April Fool's Day decorating to brighten up the party room.

Cut clown faces and hats out of colored poster paper. Paint features on the faces and then paste the hats and faces together. Paste a ruffle of bright-colored crepe paper under the chin. Make the arms of straightened wire hangers. Attach the arms to the back of the head with gummed tape. Cover the arms with crepe-paper fringe of another color. Fasten some balloons to the hands. Hung above doors and windows, these clowns are very effective and gay.

CLOWN CENTERPIECE

Using ink, paint a face on a blown-up, light-colored balloon. Tie the string that fastens the balloon stem to a 10-inch circle of cardboard. Paste a paper clown hat to the balloon head and make a crepe-paper ruffle to go around the neck.

MERRY-GO-ROUND CENTERPIECE

This effective merry-go-round takes about ten minutes to make. It has colored figures of amusing animals and people, cut from magazines.

The revolving part of the merry-go-round is a paper plate. Push a nail through the exact center of the plate so that the point is underneath. Then glue a square of lightweight cardboard over the nail.

Glue one end of an empty spool to a piece of heavy cardboard about 5 inches square. Then put the nail into the hole at the opposite end of the spool. The plate will now spin around as fast or slowly as you wish.

Cut out pictures of circus animals and people, paste them on cardboard and cut around the edges. Make a tab at the bottom of each piece of cardboard to fold over and glue to the merry-go-round.

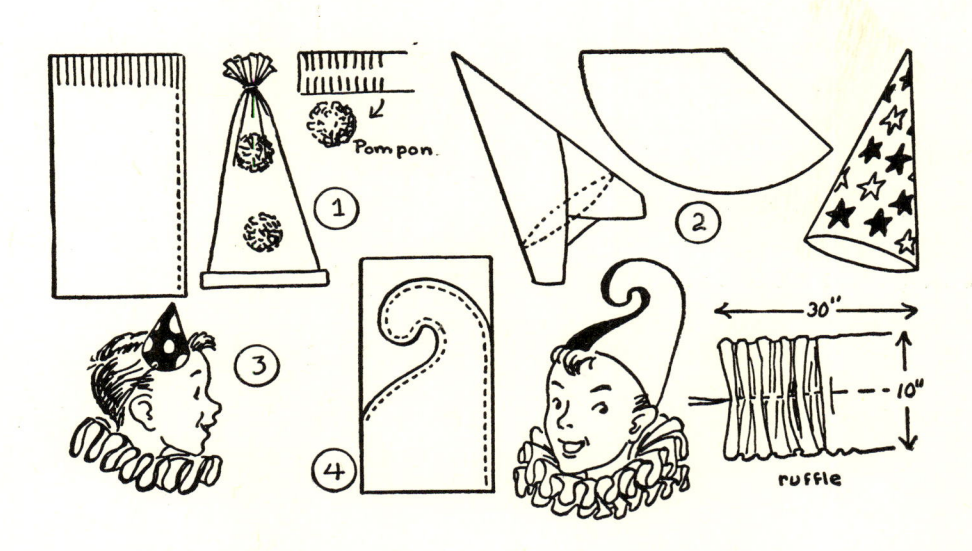

PAPER CLOWN HATS

Here are four easy-to-make clown hats. Your guests will enjoy wearing them.

(1) Cut a strip of crepe paper the width of the fold of the paper (20 inches) and 23 inches long. Fold it in half. Sew the side edges together. Fringe the top and tie it with a string. Turn up the bottom edge one inch. Paste two different colored pompons on the front of the hat.

(2) Make a cone of stiff, colored paper (you may use the Sunday

APRIL FOOL'S DAY

comics if you wish). Paste the edges of the cone together after you have adjusted the hat to fit your head. Paste colored paper stars on the stiff paper hat.

(3) Make small cones of colored construction paper. Decorate them with painted or pasted-on colored dots. Tie the hat on your head with string or thread elastic.

(4) This hat is made of two thicknesses of crepe paper. Cut four pieces of crepe paper 20 inches (the width of the paper) by 12 inches. Use two pieces of one color and two of another. Pin the four pieces of paper together. Cut them as shown in the diagram. Sew the edges together, leaving the bottom open. Turn the hat inside out. Turn in the bottom edge one inch.

To make your guests feel truly court-jesterish, make some neck ruffles for them. Run a basting stitch of strong double thread down the middle of a strip of colored crepe paper 10 inches by 30 inches. Gather the paper on the string. Leave the thread long enough to tie around the neck. Be sure to have a big knot on the ends of the thread. Pull the edges of the crepe paper gently to make it ruffly.

STRAW-SIPPING PLACE CARDS

Draw a clown on heavy white drawing paper or bristol board as shown in the diagram. Color him with bright crayon colors. Cut around the dark outline carefully and punch a hole in his mouth big enough to hold a drinking straw. Write your guest's name on the collar and place the sipping clown on a glass of pink lemonade.

THE ENDLESS THREAD

Try this stunt at your party or when you are with a group of friends. Get a spool of white or colored thread, and thread the free end through a needle. Put the spool in a side coat pocket. Then pass the needle through the cloth on the inside of your coat, and out to the front of your coat, as shown in the drawing. Remove the needle, and leave an inch or so of the thread on the front of your coat.

Someone is pretty sure to see the thread and try to tidy you up by removing it. When they do, the fun starts. The thread keeps coming out through your coat as if it were endless.

CARDBOARD POPEYES

You will need a fairly heavy white cardboard, such as is used for shoe boxes, for these amusing popeyes.

Cut two oval pieces, each 1¼ inches long and 1 inch wide. Soak these pieces in water for a little while and then place one oval in the bowl of a spoon. On each piece, place another spoon and press them together to shape the cardboard into a curved shape. Put books on the spoons to weight them down, or tie the spoons together, and leave them until the cardboard is dry.

Once dry, paint the eyes in the funniest ways you can. Use ink and water colors or crayons. Cut a hole in each eye, being careful to put it where you can see through it when you are wearing the eyes. Also make a very small hole in the inner and upper corner of each eye. Fasten a piece of stiff wire through these holes to fit across the bridge of your nose and hold the eyes on.

You can also have fun with one eye fastened to a black string and used as a monocle.

APRIL FOOL'S DAY

MAGIC MENAGERIE

A good April Fool's Day stunt for your party is a magic menagerie. The menagerie is a box into which you invite your friends to look. You tell them that they will see in the box any animal they care to name.

The box is a cardboard carton with an old mirror in the back. Turn the box on its side, and place the mirror flat against the inside back. Drape a large cloth or scarf around the box and let part of the cloth hang down over the open front.

Each person is asked what animal he would like to see in the box. When he has named the animal, you remove the cloth and let him look in the mirror. If he has chosen to see a monkey, there is the monkey in the mirror!

PAPER CUP RACING PLANES

With a snip of a pair of scissors, you can make a pointed paper-cup into a racing plane that flies along a piece of string. Just cut off the pointed tip at the bottom, as in the diagram. You can also use a paper cup shaped like a regular drinking glass. To make the cup ride the string, punch a small hole in its bottom, close up against the edge.

If you wish to, you can paste paper wings to the cups to make them look more like airplanes.

Make two planes so that two people can race against each other. Put up two pieces of string, each the length of a room. Thread the planes on the strings before you fasten them to the wall with thumbtacks or tacks. Then, at the word "Go," each person starts to blow his plane along the string. The winner is the one whose plane is the first to touch the opposite wall.

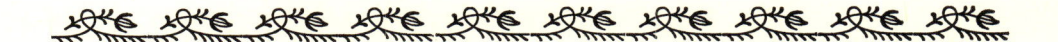

ARBOR DAY

The date of Arbor Day varies from State to State, but April is a good time to plant trees. The ground is soft from the melting of the snow and the roots can spread out and absorb the goodness of the earth. It is warm enough for the sap to flow and carry nourishment to all parts of the tree. This Arbor Day, plant an acorn or a maple seed somewhere on your lawn.

It is fun to grow things indoors, too. If you have no lawn or backyard, plant something indoors at home or at school. Invite your friends to join you.

Here are some amusing and interesting plants you and your friends can start. Each person may then take home his experiments. After that you will have weeks of fun, watching your plants grow and comparing notes with your friends.

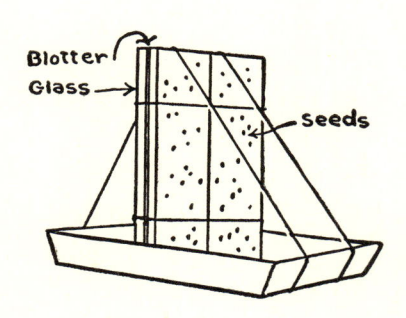

BLOTTER AND SEED EXPERIMENT

This is an interesting blotter experiment that will enable you to watch the growth of the roots of a seed.

Get two small, flat pieces of glass and a piece of brown or other dark-colored blotter to place between them, like a sandwich. Before you make the "sandwich," scatter some radish seeds on the surface of the blotter.

Bind up the "sandwich" with rubber bands or string. Then stand it upright in a pan, and fasten it to the pan with string or rubber bands so it will not fall over.

Then pour a little water into the pan. The water will gradually seep up into the blotter, dampening the seeds between the pieces of glass. As soon as the seeds receive the moisture, they will begin to sprout. Watching your "sandwich" through the glass from day to day, you will be able to see the growth of the roots.

A POTATO PORCUPINE

You can have fun with a Potato Porcupine for a long time, because it takes time for his bristles to grow, and it is fun to watch them sprout a little more each day.

Make the body from a well-shaped potato. Scoop out the inside with a knife, leaving plenty of good solid potato on the sides and bottom. Make the eyes from beads or buttons and pin them in place. Use bits of wooden matches or whittled scraps of wood for feet. These can be easily inserted in the body of the porcupine.

The bristles are mustard plants, which you can buy at almost any florist's shop. Plant them on a piece of well-moistened cotton placed in the hollow which you have scooped out of the potato. Water the cotton a little each day and in a few days the plants will sprout into a crop of luxuriant green bristles.

EGGSHELL FLOWER POTS

Eggshells make good little flower pots. Save the shells after someone in the family has baked a cake or scrambled eggs. Rinse out the bottom halves of the shells and fill them with earth. Then plant a grapefruit seed, a flower seed, an appleseed or a bean in each shell. Put each shell in an egg cup or a small glass and put them on a windowsill where they will have sun and air.

SWEET POTATO INDOOR GARDEN

One of the easiest ways to keep attractive, growing things in your room is to plant several sweet potatoes in glasses of water. They sprout very quickly and will soon send green, leafy trailers over the side of the glass. Put the glass on a shelf or windowsill where the trailer will have room to grow downward.

BOTTLE GARDENS

Bottle gardens, which you can watch grow, are always interesting and will last for a long time. To make one, use a good-sized bottle or jar with a wide mouth. Rest it on one side and put in it a foundation of pebbles and sand to take care of drainage. Cover this with rich earth, filling the jar to nearly half its diameter. Cut a half circle of cardboard to fit against the dirt at the neck of the jar to keep it from dropping out. Wet the sand and earth before putting them in the bottle.

Then, with a pair of tweezers or a thin stick, plant seeds here and there in the earth. Sprinkle grass seed over the top of the earth to make a lawn. Grapefruit seeds will grow into graceful little trees. You can also plant orange, lemon and appleseeds, and a small piece of horse-radish may be cut and planted to grow into a hedge fence. Any kind of flower seed that produces tiny leaves can be used. Maple and elm seedlings make good trees.

Water your garden sparingly with a bulb spray. If the earth is soaked with water the seeds will rot. The plants need both air and moisture, and the best way to regulate the atmosphere is to perforate the lid or cap of the jar and to cork the bottle some of the time to prevent evaporation. By careful observation you will learn how much is needed.

You can add little houses or human figures to the garden, if you wish to.

MAY DAY

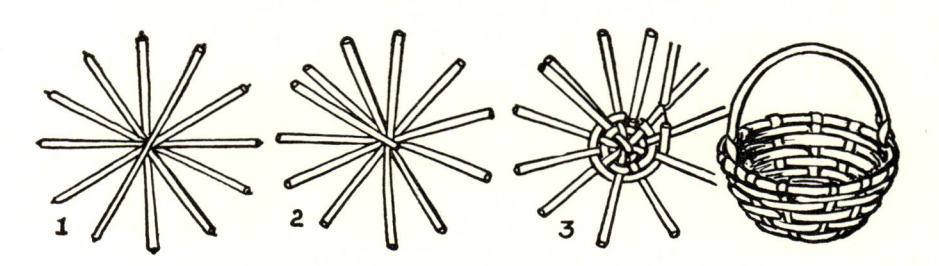

SODA-STRAW MAY BASKETS

      The first of May is May Day, a gay outdoor holiday. In parks everywhere you will see May queens, May poles, dancing children, flowers and May baskets.

      Giving May baskets is a charming old custom. Boys and girls gather wild flowers—or make paper flowers—and put them into little baskets to give to friends. Here is an unusual May basket you can make to fill and give to someone.

      These baskets are made of plain or colored soda straws, eight pieces of wire, same length as straws, and some colored yarn.

      Start by putting six pieces of wire through six straws. Then arrange the straws as in drawing 1. Next, twist them around each other at the center until they are held together, as in drawing 2.

      Get a long piece of colored yarn. Make a small loop at the end of the two remaining pieces of wire. Thread the yarn through the loop. Then, using the wire as a needle, string onto the yarn fifteen straws, and make a knot at the end of the yarn to keep the straws in place. Use colored straws if you can get them. When all the straws are in place, remove the wire needle.

      Tie one end of the yarn to the center of the six straws. Then start weaving the straws strung on the yarn over and under the six straws, as in drawing 3. When you come to the end of a straw, wind the yarn twice around the next straw to hold it securely, and then go on with the weaving.

When you have woven enough to make the bottom of the basket, bend the six straws upward to shape the sides. Continue to weave, but twist the weaving straw once around each straw in the sides as you come to it. When all fifteen straws have been woven into place, tie the end of the yarn to the straw it reaches.

Make the top rim of the basket by covering the eighth wire with a straw and twisting the ends of the six side straws around it. Then make a handle by slipping the wire used as a needle through a straw and fastening it to each side by twisting the wire around two of the side straws.

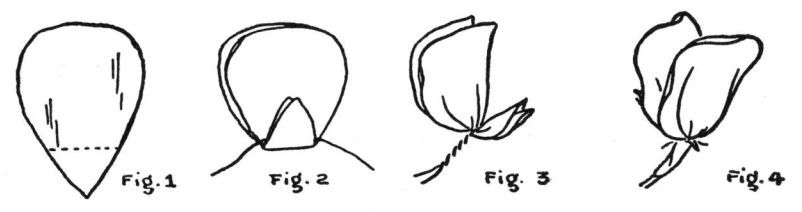

CREPE-PAPER SWEET PEAS

To fill your May basket, make some crepe-paper sweet peas. These are one of the most popular and easiest to make of all the crepe-paper flowers. A bunch of paper sweet peas can be made to look so much like the real flowers that from a distance people can hardly tell the difference. Good colors to use are pink, lavender and white.

To make a sweet pea, cut two petals of crepe paper in the shape shown in Fig. 1, being sure to have the grain of the paper up and down. Make each of these pieces a little more than 2 inches long.

Cut a piece of thin green wire about 8 inches long. Hold the two petals together with their edges exactly even with each other. Fold their bottom points upward and place the piece of wire in the fold, as shown in Fig. 2, putting the center of the wire at the center of the petal. Then pull the ends of the wire tightly together to draw the petals into a ruffle, as in Fig. 3. Twist the wire to form a stem, and then press the small ends of the petals to make them curve upward.

Now press one of the big petals backward, so that it hangs over the two small ends. Turn the other large petal carefully in the opposite direction. This completes the flower. To make it still more lifelike, wrap the wire stem with a narrow strip of green crepe paper.

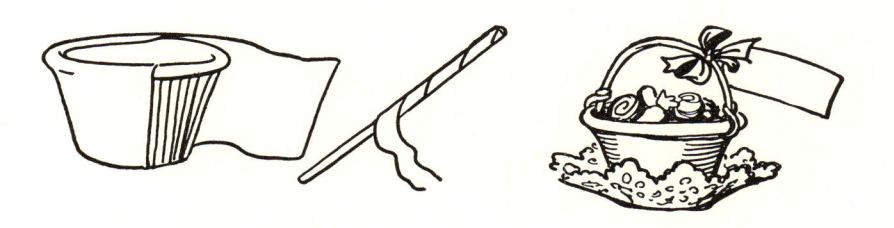

NUT-CUP PARTY BASKETS

May parties are held indoors, too, complete with May baskets, May poles, games and fun. Basket favors for your May Day party are easy to make.

You will need colored crepe paper (any flower color), paper nut cups, small lace paper doilies and some fairly heavy wire. Cut a strip of crepe paper ¼ inch wider than the depth of the cup. Cut the paper across the grain. Brush the outside of the cup lightly with white paste and gently stretch the paper around the cup. Allow the extra ¼ inch of paper to fold over the top of the cup.

Wind a narrow strip of crepe paper around a 6-inch piece of wire. Bend the wire to form the handle. Cut 2 holes opposite each other just below the rim of the basket and insert the ends of the wire handle, twisting them in place as in the drawing. Tie a name card to the handle and make a ribbon bow. Paste the basket to a small paper doily and fill it with colored candies.

MAY POLE CENTERPIECE

For this centerpiece you will need a ⅜-inch dowel stick 12 inches long, a large spool and a small spool, heavy cardboard, colored crepe paper, glue and paste.

Cut two circles from the cardboard, one 4½ inches in diameter and the other 10 inches in diameter.

Whittle the ends of the dowel stick until one spool fits on each end. To keep the spools firmly in place, put a little glue on the ends of the

MAY DAY

stick before inserting them in the spools. Wrap narrow strips of colored crepe paper around the spools and stick and paste the ends in place.

Glue the small cardboard circle to the top of the small spool and the large circle to the bottom of the large spool. Color the circles green with tempera paint or cover them with green crepe paper.

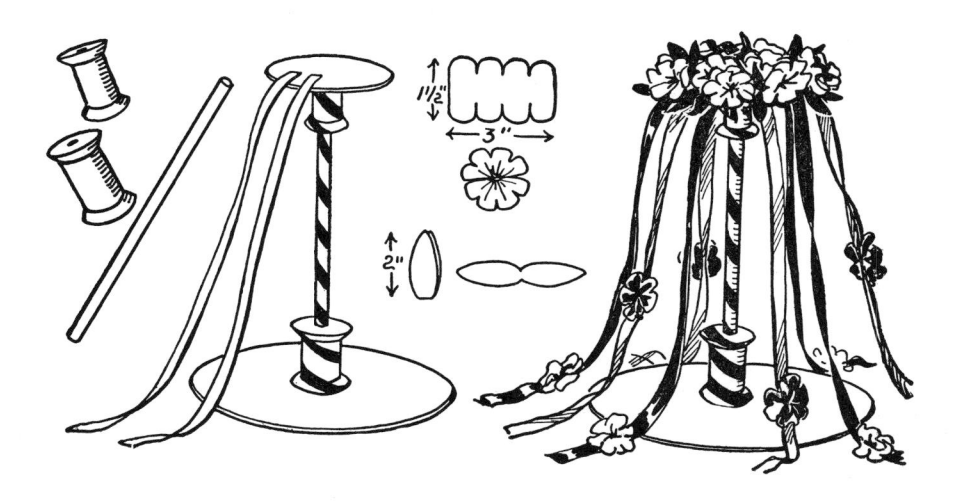

Paste narrow crepe-paper strips 16 inches long to the small disk, as in the drawing. Use several different colors.

Make colored crepe-paper flowers and leaves as shown in the diagram. Paste them around the edge and on the top of the small disk. Paste a few flowers to the streamers. Then place the May pole in the center of the table, allowing the streamers to trail over the tablecloth.

MAY DAY PARTY HATS

Of course there should be a May king and a May queen at your party. Their crowns are easily made of cardboard covered with gold paper, with colored-paper jewels pasted on.

Flower hats are easy to make and are very effective. Cut a strip of crepe paper, using any flower color, the full width of the crepe paper and 22 inches long. Fold this strip in half, lengthwise. Stitch the seam up the back. The folded edge is the bottom. Cut the petals at the top edge about 4 inches deep. From yellow or black crepe paper cut a fringe center, as in the drawing. Insert the center among the petals and tie them together with a bit of wire or string. Spread out the petals. Stretch the center of each petal gently to make it cup.

Robin Hood was an outdoor man, so make Robin Hood hats for the active young men at your party. They are made of a double thickness of green crepe paper. Use 2 sheets, each 17 inches wide and 22 inches long. Place one sheet on top of the other and fold them, as in the drawing. Pin the edges together and cut the top as shown. Sew the back and top edges with green thread. Stretch the bottom edge a little and turn up the brim. The feathers are made of two thicknesses of colored construction paper pasted together.

CRAYON ART CLASS

This is a party stunt bound to produce good laughs.

Supply each person with a large sheet of paper and a black crayon and allow ten minutes in which everyone must draw a caricature of someone in the room. The idea is to make the pictures look as much as possible like the model, but to make them comical by exaggeration.

When the ten minutes are up, collect and number all the drawings and either hang them on the wall or spread them on a table. Each person is then given a piece of paper and told to write on it the number of each picture and the name of the person they think it is meant to represent.

The person who correctly guesses the largest number of pictures is the winner. Another winner can be the person who drew the picture identified by the greatest number of people.

MOTHER'S DAY

A. PAPER CARNATION

                        The second Sunday in May is Mother's Day and the carnation is the flower which symbolizes it. These flowers are easily made in only a few minutes.

    The diagram shows the exact size of one fourth of the flower pattern. Trace and cut out this pattern. Fold a 4½-inch square of pink crepe paper in quarters, place the pattern on the folded paper and cut out the petals. Cut 3 more circles of petals. Pleat or score each petal with a scissors blade or your fingernail. Gather the petals in the center and tie all four bunches of petals together with wire, as in the drawing. Wrap a strip of green crepe paper around the base of the flower and the wire stem.

    Pin the carnation to a card with your greetings to your mother, or use it to decorate the gift you have made for her.

MOTHER'S DAY

BUTTERFLY FLOWER HOLDER

Here is another unusual and attractive flower holder to make for Mother's Day. It is made from a five-cent test tube—a little straight-sided bottle—that you can buy at any drugstore. The test tube forms the butterfly's body. It is fastened to cardboard wings by two wires. These pass through small holes in the cardboard and are twisted together at the back. Make the butterfly 11 inches wide and 8 inches high.

A 5-inch-long test tube is a good size to use. Before putting it in place, paint the butterfly's wings yellow, white and black. Then glue two wires to them to represent the butterfly's feelers. The holder can be hung on a wall by making a wire loop at the back.

CARDBOARD FLOWER GIRL

This is an unusual and attractive flower-holding gadget for you to put at your mother's place on the breakfast table on Mother's Day. The flower girl holds fresh flowers in her hands.

Draw the figure of the girl on heavy cardboard. Make her about 6½ inches tall. Cut the figure out and color it with paints or crayons. You do not have to draw the hands, since they will be hidden by the flowers. Then cut a ¾-inch hole in the center, as shown in the drawing. Put some water in a glass and stand the flower girl against it. Then push the stems of the flowers she is to hold through the hole and into the glass.

FLAG DAY

June 14 is Flag Day, the birthday of our flag. On that day in 1777 the Continental Congress declared, "The flag of the United States shall have 13 stripes of alternate red and white with a union of 13 stars of white in a blue field."

Betsy Ross made the first American flag. It was a beautiful flag with red and white stripes and a circle of white stars on a blue ground.

Now we have 48 stars on our flag, one for each state in the Union. We still have 13 stripes to remind us of the 13 original colonies.

FLAG DAY DECORATIONS

Let's have a Betsy Ross party this Flag Day. Decorate the doors and windows with bands of blue crepe paper with white or silver stars. Make festoons and hangings of two-inch strips of red and white crepe paper. To cut the strips easily, see general instructions, page 12.

For the table centerpiece, stick little flags into your party cake, one for each guest. These little flags can be bought by the package in most ten-cent stores. When the cake is cut everyone is given a piece of cake with a flag.

FLAG DAY

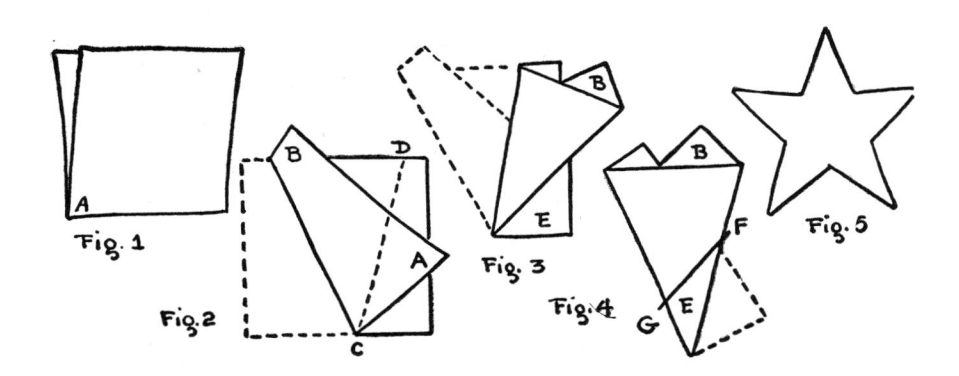

HOW TO CUT A FIVE-POINTED STAR

You can make a perfect five-pointed star with one snip of a pair of scissors by following these directions. You may want to make some for fun or for Flag Day decorations.

Take a piece of paper twice as long as it is wide—for example, 10 inches long by 5 inches wide. Fold it upward along the center line to make Fig. 1. Fold the corner A over, as in Fig. 2. Fold B over along the dotted line CD to make Fig. 3. Fold corner E over from right to left to make Fig. 4. Then cut along the straight line FG. Open out the small cut-off piece and you will have your star.

PARTY HATS

BETSY ROSS CAP

(1) Cut a strip of white crepe paper the width of the crepe paper fold (20 inches) and 24 inches long. Sew a 4½-inch strip to the short side. You now have a 24-inch square.

(2) Fold the square in half, then in quarters, then in eighths and cut the edge as shown in the diagram. You now have a large circle.

(3) Use strong double thread to gather the circle 1½ inches from the edge to fit the head. Fasten the ends of the thread securely. A yard of 1-inch-wide red or blue ribbon tied with a bow over the stitching completes the cap.

COLONIAL HATS

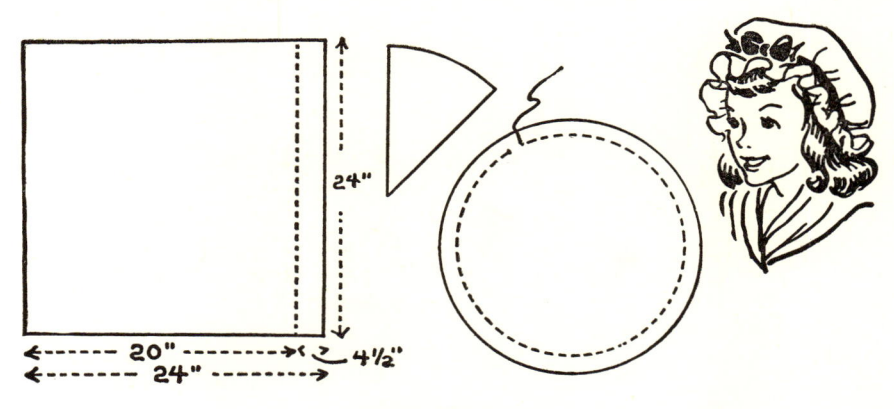

(1) For Colonial hats you will need large sheets of heavy black mat stock. Cut a strip of paper 3 inches wide and 23 inches long. Sew the short ends together to fit the head. Press the sides in to make it slightly oval. This is the crown.

(2) Draw and cut out a circle 14 inches in diameter for the brim.

(3) Place the crown in the center of the brim and draw a line on the brim around the crown.

(4) Remove the crown and cut out the center part of the brim 1 inch inside the crown line. Then, every inch, cut a slit in as far as the crown line.

(5) Turn up the flaps on the inside of the brim and sew the crown to the flaps.

(6) Turn up the brim on three sides and staple or tack the brim to the crown. Paste a red, white and blue cockade to one side.

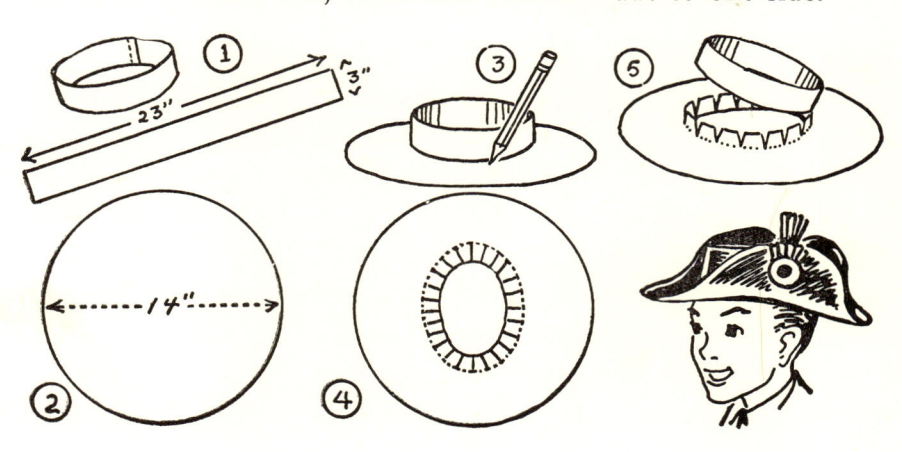

FLAG DAY

UNUSUAL BUTTON PLACE CARDS

These attractive button place cards will be fun to have at your party. You can make all kinds of different faces and figures.

Use white or light-colored buttons that have two holes in them. The holes are the eyes. Cut the bodies out of cardboard, using the shapes in the pictures or creating your own, and glue the button faces to them. Then dress the little figures by gluing pieces of different kinds of cloth to them. Cut the cloth to the right shape to make shirts, blouses, hats, capes, bows, etc. You can use felt, velvet, lace, taffeta and feathers to create all kinds of different costumes. The features of the faces are put on with water colors.

CREPE-PAPER CUTTING RACE

This is a good indoor party stunt, but you can try it out of doors as well. Take two crepe-paper streamers, each ten feet long and 1 inch wide, and pin one end of each to an upholstered chair. If you are playing outdoors, attach the streamers to a tree. Two contestants, each provided with a pair of scissors, hold the free ends of the streamers and stand 10 feet away from the chair or tree.

At the word "Go," each contestant starts to cut along the center line of his or her streamer. A contestant is disqualified if he cuts through a side of his streamer or drops the streamer to the floor. The first to cut his streamer into two narrow strips is the winner.

FATHER'S DAY

STRING HOLDER

A funnel string holder is an unusual and useful gift that you can make to give to your father on Father's Day, which comes on the third Sunday in June. It is very easy to make and, when attractively painted, it is a really good-looking and useful gadget to use in a workshop.

Any funnel large enough to hold a ball of string can be used. Enamel the funnel red, green, blue or any color you choose. Then add a decalcomania of a horse or dog or whatever you wish. Or you can use colored pictures from magazines.

The end of the ball of string hangs down through the funnel.

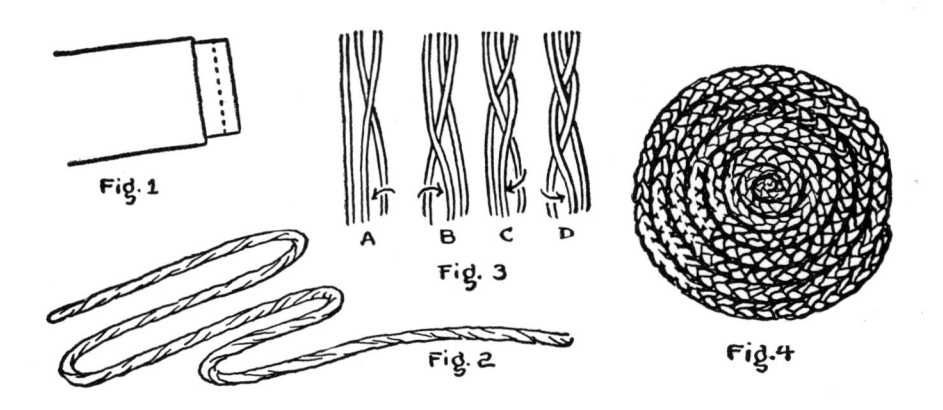

CREPE-PAPER COASTERS AND MATS

Another useful gift to make for your father is a coaster or mat to put under his tobacco jar to keep it from scratching the table. These coasters or mats are attractive and durable and are interesting to make.

Start with a package of crepe paper. Slide one end out from the cover and cut off the paper one inch from the edge. Unfold the cut-off part and twist it tightly into a rope.

Cut this rope into three equal lengths. These are to be braided together. Tie them together at one end and fasten them to a table with thumbtacks or with a weight.

Fig. 3 shows how to braid the three strands together. Bring the right outside strand over the center strand, as in A. Bring the left outside strand over the center strand, as at B. Bring the right outside strand over the center, as at C. Bring the left outside strand over the center, as at D. Continue in the same way, bringing the right strand over the center, then the left, then the right, and so on.

When the braid is completed, coil it tightly to form a mat, as in Fig. 4. Sew the edges together with a simple over-and-under stitch. Finish by applying a coat of thin shellac, followed by a second coat the following day.

THE FOURTH OF JULY

On the Fourth of July in 1776, the Declaration of Independence was signed and our country was born. Ever since, the Fourth of July has been an exciting holiday with parades, fireworks, picnics and parties.

Here are a few ideas for gadgets and games for a Fourth of July picnic.

PAPER FIRECRACKERS

Paper firecrackers go off with a bang loud enough to make most people jump. You can make one in less than a minute, and you will find that they are safe and fun to use.

Take a piece of good quality typewriter paper, stiff letter paper or heavy wrapping paper about 8 inches square. Fold it as in Fig. 2, so the bottom edge comes to within an inch of the top edge. Then fold one side over on the other along the dotted center line to make Fig. 3.

Turn the paper upside down and hold it by corners A and B, between your right thumb and forefinger. Then swing your forearm and hand down very quickly. As the air rushes in and opens out the paper, the firecracker will explode with a noise like a pistol shot.

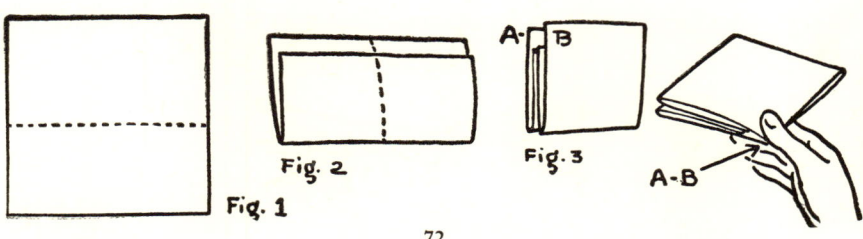

THE FOURTH OF JULY

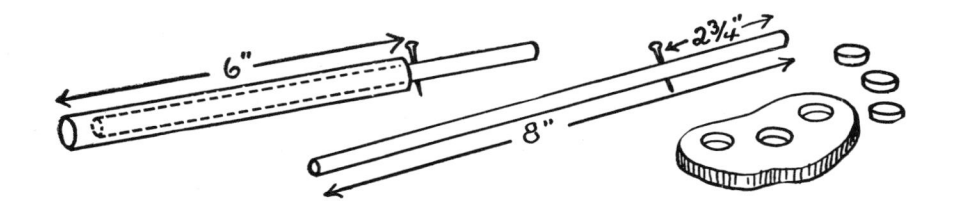

A POTATO POPGUN

Another good Fourth of July gadget is a potato popgun. This is an unusual kind of a popgun that makes a lot of noise.

Make the barrel from a piece of tin tubing 6 inches long and about ¾ inch in diameter. You can get this at a hardware store or you can use a short section of a peashooter.

Fit the barrel with a wooden plunger that fits snugly inside the tube, but can be pushed easily in and out. A piece of smooth dowel wood, which you can get at a hardware store, is just right for the plunger. Make it about 8 inches long, and drive a thin nail through it at a point 2¾ inches from one end.

To fire the gun, make potato ammunition. Cut a potato into slices ⅛ inch thick. Plug one end of the popgun barrel tight by pushing it through a slice of potato. Then reverse the tube and plug the other end in the same manner. Push the plunger slowly into one end of the barrel until the potato plug in that end is an inch or so from the end. Then slam the plunger home at full speed. The compression of the air inside the tube will force the other plug out with a bang.

CLOTHESPIN GLIDERS

You can make these gliders in a couple of minutes and have fun throwing them through the air. If some of your friends make some, too, you can race to see who can make his glider go farthest or highest.

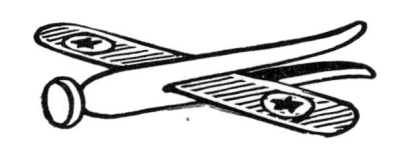

Each glider consists of a clothespin fitted with a wing cut from shirt cardboard from the laundry or other lightweight cardboard. Wedge the wing in with paper or small bits of wood if it doesn't fit tightly enough. You can paint the gliders different colors, if you wish.

CREPE-PAPER SWIRLERS

You can have a good deal of fun with one of these brightly colored swirlers, making spirals, figure eights and other figures by whirling it around.

To make a three-colored swirler, get three packages of crepe paper, each a different color. Without unfolding the packages, cut two strips off the end of each one. Make the strips about ¾ inch wide.

Unfold each strip, and fold it into four parts of equal length. Hold the four sections together, as in the drawing, and pull on the ends to stretch the paper. Do this with all six strips. Then put the strips side by side and tie them together at one end, tying in a weight such as a heavy nut or several metal washers. The weight makes the swirler work better.

Tie the swirler to a string about 5 feet long. Hold the string by the free end and whirl the swirler around your head in circles and figure eights.

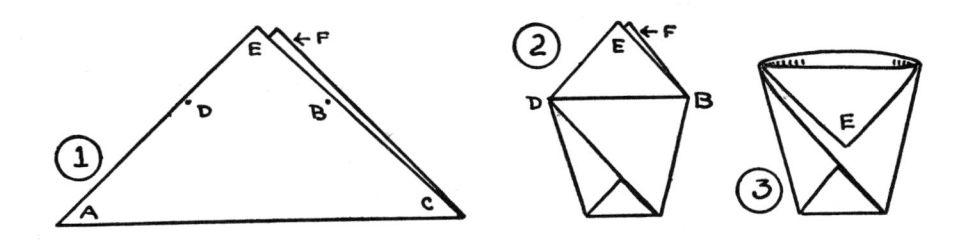

HOW TO MAKE A PAPER CUP

You might run short of paper cups at your picnic, so it is useful to know how to make one. The drawings show how to make a first-class, water-tight paper cup by making a few folds in a piece of paper. Cut a piece of stiff paper about 8 inches square. Fold it from corner to corner, as in drawing 1. Fold corner A to point B, and corner C to point D. The paper will then appear as in drawing 2. To complete the cup, fold corners E and F down over the sides.

THE ALPHABET GAME

This is a grand game for a large group and is especially good for the Fourth of July since it can be played in or out of doors.

Print two sets of alphabet cards on pieces of heavy drawing paper or cardboard. The cards should be fairly large—about 9 by 12 inches. Print one letter on each card, making one set red and one set black. If you have fewer than fifty-two people, print Q and U on one card and X, Y and Z on another.

The girls can be the red team and the boys the black. The teams line up on opposite sides of the room or lawn. The free ends of the field are marked with a tape or chalk line goal, the red goal at one end and the black at the other. A set of alphabet cards is then distributed to each team, and each person must hold his card so that it can be seen at all times.

A caller (who is not on either team) calls out a word, and all the people holding the letters of that word rush to their team's goal line and arrange themselves to spell the word. The team that spells the word correctly first wins a point. The letters all go back to their places and another word is called, and so on. The team that gets five points first wins the game.

The caller should find long words in which the letters are used only once, and it is more fun if unusual words, using many different letters, are used. This gives everyone a chance to play. Here are a few examples: kitchen, musical, yachting, culinary, zenith, azimuth, weight, Columbia.

Another good game for a Fourth of July picnic is the familiar and time-worn favorite, the potato race.

COLUMBUS DAY DECORATIONS

COLUMBUS DAY

COLUMBUS DAY DECORATIONS

We celebrate Columbus Day on October 12, the day, in 1492, when Columbus, with his little fleet of three tiny ships landed for the first time on American soil after an adventurous voyage over unknown seas.

Columbus Day decorations can be unusual and colorful. Cutouts of Columbus's ship, the Santa Maria, the red, white and gold flag of old Spain, anchors, whales and sea serpents are all good motifs to use.

The cutouts are made of mat stock or large sheets of colored construction paper. The Spanish flag has gold castles on a white ground and red lions on a white ground. The ships should be black when they are placed near the red whales and sea serpents and red when they are combined with the black anchors. Make the waves of green crepe paper cut through the entire fold of the paper.

Make a half-size cutout of the ship to decorate your party cake. Fasten it in place with toothpicks. A scalloped ring of green construction paper around the cake can be the sea.

COLUMBUS DAY PARTY HATS

You can make a number of different kinds of hats for Columbus Day: crowns for King Ferdinand and Queen Isabella, a large one for him and a small one for her; Indian headbands; and tasseled caps that Spanish sailors of old might have worn.

The crowns are cardboard over which is pasted gold or silver paper. Paste on bits of colored paper to make the jewels.

The feathers of the Indian bands are cut out of two thicknesses of colored construction paper and pasted together. Make the headbands of colored cloth or a folded piece of crepe paper.

The tasseled caps are red or green crepe paper with gold tassels. They are made from a piece of paper 20 inches wide and 22 inches long, folded in half. Stitch the seam at the back. Tie a little fringe of crepe paper to the top. Turn the bottom up one inch, and the cap is finished.

WALNUT SHELL BOAT PLACE CARDS

It is surprising what effective little ships can be made by using walnut shells for the hulls and matches or toothpicks for the masts and bowsprits. The drawings show several kinds, all of which are easy to make. Paste these walnut boats to cards on which your guests' names are written and you will have unusual place cards for your Columbus Day party.

The masts are held upright by gluing two matchsticks or other pieces of wood across the shell on both sides of them. The bowsprits are pieces of toothpick or wooden matchsticks whittled to a point. Cut sails from bits of paper and glue them to the top of the mast and to the top of the bowsprit or attach them to a thread running from the top of the mast to the end of the bowsprit.

When taken off the place cards these little boats are fun to sail on a pond or in a bathtub.

COLUMBUS DAY

HOW TO STAND AN EGG ON END

This is the trick that Columbus is said to have shown to Queen Isabella of Spain, when she told him it was impossible that the earth was round. "It is also considered impossible to stand an egg on one end," said Columbus, "but I will show you that it can be done."

With that, he picked up an egg and shook it thoroughly for a minute or two. The shaking broke the yoke. Columbus allowed the broken yoke to settle in the large end of the egg and stood the egg upright on that end. When you do this stunt, be sure to put the egg on a table that has a cloth on it.

POTATO PUPPETS

Entertain your guests with a puppet show. If you make a couple of potato puppets you can make them wave their arms, nod their heads and crack jokes with each other—with yourself acting the role of ventriloquist. The puppets can be Columbus and Queen Isabella.

Pick two potatoes that have bumps and indentations that make them look like faces. Give them thumbtack eyes, and cut a hole in the bottom of each head, so you can put your first finger inside the potato. Paint the hair on with ink. The paper crown and hat are attached to the head with pins.

Make costumes from small paper bags. Cut a hole in the center of the bottom of the bag for your first finger. Then cut a hole in each side of the bag near the bottom corners. Your thumb and second finger go through these holes to form the puppet's arms. Decorate the paper bag costumes with crayons. After you put the bag over your hand, ask someone to tie a piece of string or ribbon around it to serve as a belt and hold the costume in place.

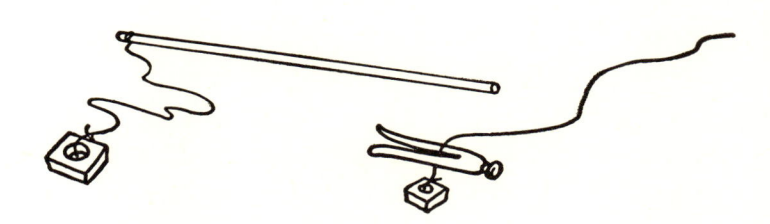

CLOTHESPIN FISH

Clothespins are first-class, ready-made fish with which to play a fishing game in a large dishpan full of water. The fishing pole is a stick with a piece of string tied to one end, and a metal nut or metal washer tied to the end of the string.

Set the clothespins afloat on the water. The stunt is to maneuver the string into the slot of a clothespin. When you succeed in doing this, you have hooked your fish and can pull him out of the water. The object of the game is to see who can hook the greatest number of fish in a given time. The time allowed is usually not more than a minute or a minute and a half.

HALLOWEEN

HALLOWEEN DECORATIONS

Goblins and ghosts, chills and thrills and fun galore—Halloween, the night when witches fly and goblins prowl, is a wonderful time to have a party.

Halloween decorations must be spooky and weird but full of fun. Make cutouts of gray ghosts, black witches, black cats, orange pumpkins and green moons. Spider webs and moss of gray crepe paper, hung with the cutouts from real branches, painted white, will give the room a fine spine-chilling effect.

Make the cutouts of black, light gray, orange and light green mat stock. To make the patterns for the figures, see general instructions, page 12.

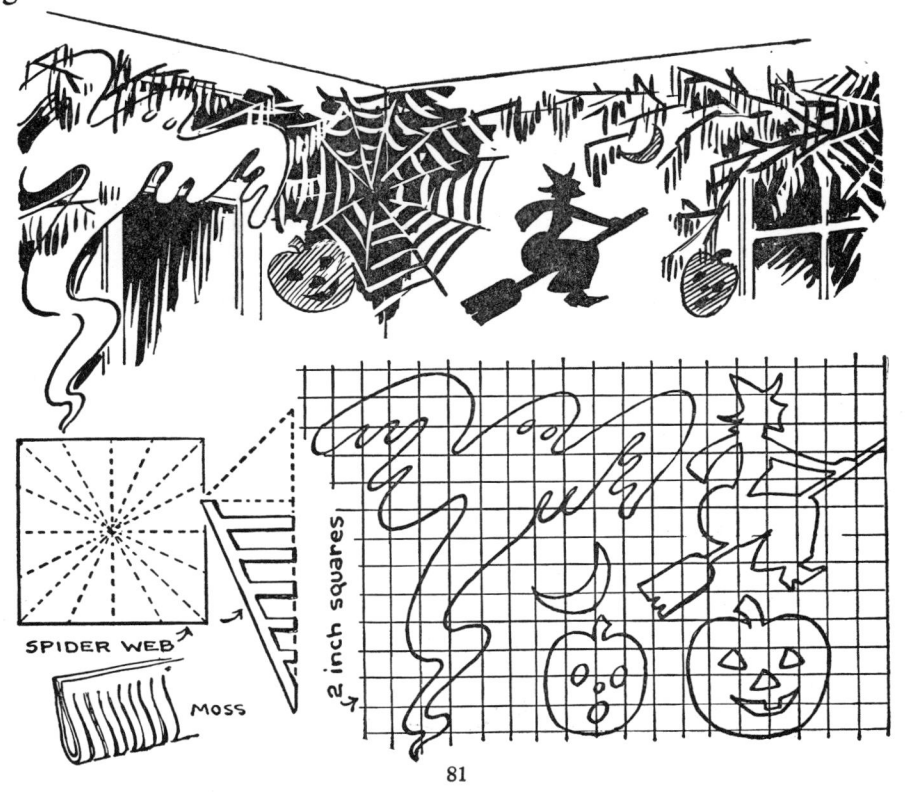

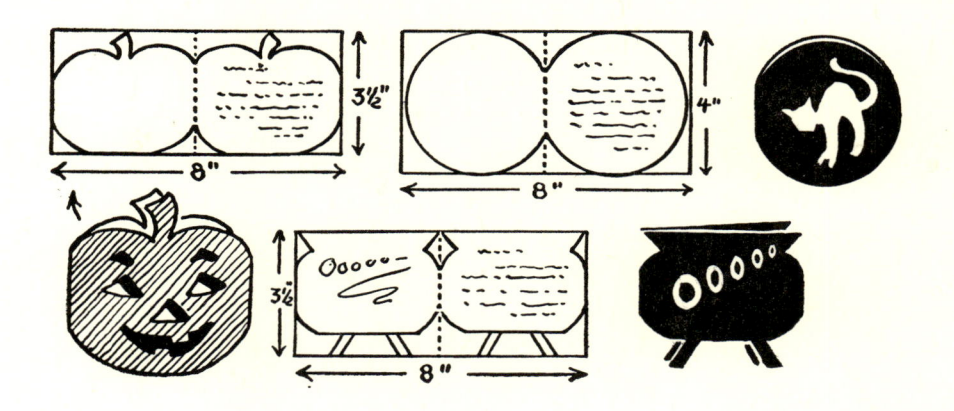

HALLOWEEN INVITATIONS

These Halloween invitations are cut out of folds of construction paper. The message is written on the inside sheet.

The pumpkin is orange with eyes, nose and mouth drawn on with black ink. The witch and the black cat are cutouts of black paper pasted to pale green moons. The witch's caldron is made of black paper and the message is written with white ink.

LOLLIPOP WITCH FAVORS

Bring the goblins and witches to your party table. These lollipop witches are fun to make.

Cover a flat lollipop with white paper and paint a witch face on it. Make the skirt and cape of one piece of black crepe paper 6 inches wide and 12 inches long. Attach it to the lollipop with a pipe cleaner. The pipe cleaner becomes the arms. One hand holds the place card and the other holds a toothpick broom that has bristles made of orange crepe paper.

Make the hat of black construction paper with a crown about 2½ inches wide and 3 inches long. Make a cone and fringe the bottom edge. The brim is a 3-inch circle with a slit in the middle. Paste the cone to the lollipop head and slip the brim over it.

HALLOWEEN 83

If the little witch won't stand up, punch a hole in the bottom of a small paper cup and push the lollipop stick into it.

PUMPKIN CENTERPIECE

This is an easy to make and effective Halloween centerpiece. All you need is orange and green crepe paper, bits of black construction paper, newspapers, scissors, paste and needle and thread.

Cut a strip of orange crepe paper the full width of the paper (20 inches) and 26 inches long. Fold it and sew the sides together. Gather the bottom and tie it securely. This is the pumpkin shell. Turn it inside out.

Make a large ball of crushed newspaper, large enough to fit into the pumpkin shell. Wrap the ball with 4-inch strips of orange crepe paper to keep it from spreading. Slip the ball into the pumpkin shell and tie the top securely. Flatten the pumpkin a little. Cut out black construction paper eyes, nose and mouth. Paste them in place.

Cut out green crepe-paper leaves. Attach a few to the stem of the pumpkin. Wind a strip of green crepe paper over the stem. Set the pumpkin in the center of the table on a bed of green leaves.

HALLOWEEN COSTUMES

Halloween is dress-up time. Wrapped in a sheet and wearing a white mask, you can give a fine ghostly greeting to your guests. Or you can be an elegant scarecrow or a ragamuffin dressed in gaily patched clothes that are too large for you. You might even be a gypsy fortuneteller draped in bright scarves and wearing all the beads you can find.

There is no end to the variety of costumes you and your guests can make and wear on Halloween. Here is a list of costumes that can be put together with very little effort:

Cat—Paper bag mask, see below. Old pajamas dyed black to which is sewn a long black cloth tail.

Mr. Pumpkin—A bag mask of orange crepe paper, a green crepe-paper leaf cape.

Witch—Black paper hat, black crepe-paper skirt and cape—and a broom.

Goblin—A light green mask, an orange hat and a bathrobe.

Pirate—A black paper patch over one eye, a curtain ring for an ear ring, a scarf tied around the head, a sash around the waist and a cardboard dagger.

PAPER-BAG MASKS

At Halloween or, for that matter, at any time when you are looking around for something to do, you may find it fun to make some paper-bag masks for yourself and your friends.

Ask the grocer for some fresh paper bags, or save used bags that are in good condition. You can make dozens of different kinds of faces with pencil, crayons or paints. You can also paste on crepe-paper hair or eyebrows, and ears or whiskers of colored construction paper. Give your imagination full rein. You will find many faces to copy in magazines and picture books. Cut holes in the bag for your eyes, nose and mouth.

PAPER-PLATE MASKS

You can make good masks very quickly and easily by using paper plates. All you have to do is draw eyes, a nose and a mouth on the outside of a paper plate. Cut these out with the point of a knife or scissors. Then decorate the face with crayons, making eyebrows, and adding hair around the upper edges of the plate. Make two small holes one on each side of the rim. Tie a piece of string or ribbon through the holes, and tie the mask around your head.

THE MISCHIEVOUS GHOSTS

If you fix your room in the way described here, and if you like this kind of fun, you can enjoy watching your friends' reactions when the "ghosts" start to play their tricks. This is a good stunt for Halloween.

All you have to do is get a spool of strong black thread and tie long pieces of thread to several different objects in the room. Tie the thread to a picture on the wall, to a book or to magazines lying on the table, to a small rug, and to any other movable but non-breakable object you think will be good to use. Lead all the threads through the door and fasten them to thumbtacks outside the door.

Now, when friends are in your room, go outside, or have a friend who is in on the secret go outside, and start to pull on the strings. If all goes well, you should have a hilarious time, for your friends will be completely mystified.

HALLOWEEN

HALLOWEEN TICKTACK

Spool ticktacks are old favorites as noisemakers on Halloween, but not everybody knows how to make one at home. To use a ticktack, you hold it against the side of a house and pull the string, and it produces a noise loud enough to suit anybody.

Get a large spool, and cut notches around the flange at each end. Cut them quite deep and make them close together. When you have done this, tie a long piece of string tightly to the middle of the spool. Wind the string around the spool.

Now get a large, long nail and slip it through the hole in the spool. The nail serves both as a handle and an axle. Put the spool against the side of a wooden house, pressing just hard enough to hold the notches against the wood. Then pull the string quickly. The spool will revolve and the notches will set up a clatter against the wood.

PAPER-AND-PENCIL MIND READING

Here is a good mind-reading stunt you can use to amuse and puzzle your friends.

Fold a small sheet of paper crosswise to form three sections of equal size, divided by creases, as in the drawing. Then ask someone to write three names on the paper, one in each section, with the most important name in the center. Ask him to tear the paper along the creases to make three pieces, to fold over each piece, and put all three into a hat. You then ask him to concentrate on the important name on the center piece while you close your eyes, reach into the hat, and bring it out.

The secret is that the center piece has two torn edges, while the end pieces have only one. Your sense of touch enables you to find the center piece.

WALNUT SHELL FORTUNE TELLING

This is a fortune-telling stunt that is lots of fun. Each guest is given a small candle (the candle should be as thick as a pencil) and a walnut shell. He marks the shell so that he can identify it. He then makes a wish and places the lighted candle directly in the center of the shell. A dab of melted candle wax will hold the candle in place. The shells are then placed in a large dishpan filled with water. If the shell capsizes and the candle is extinguished, the owner's wish will not come true. Those whose shells remain upright are the fortunate ones, for their wishes are supposed to come true.

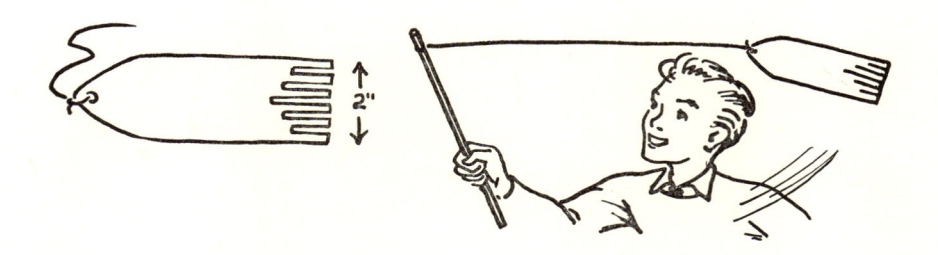

WIND-PADDLE MOANERS

(See drawing on facing page)

This is a device used by American Indians in their ceremonial dances. The paddles make a weird moaning noise when you whirl them rapidly around above your head. When several boys work their wind paddles at the same time, the noise effects are extraordinary. This is a fine gadget for Halloween.

The easiest way to make a moaner is to use thin wood from orange crates. You should be able to get some at the nearest grocery store. Cut the moaner to the shape shown in the drawing. Make it 7 inches long and 2 inches wide. Cut three $\frac{1}{8}$-inch slots in the tail end, making the center one 1¾ inches long, and two others about 1 inch long. The drawing shows five slots, but you can add the other two later or make another moaner with five slots. It will have a different tone.

Fasten the moaner to a stick about 18 inches long, using a piece of strong string 2 feet long. Then whirl the moaner around above your head. Be sure you have plenty of free space around you before you begin to whirl.

THANKSGIVING DAY

The Pilgrims landed in Plymouth in December 1620. Those who survived that first hard winter celebrated their first American harvest in October 1621. They invited the friendly Indians to join them in their Thanksgiving festivities, and all together they celebrated for three days with prayer, games and plenty of good food—wild turkey, fish, corn bread, fruits and vegetables. Today we celebrate Thanksgiving Day on the last Thursday in November, by Presidential proclamation. For us, too, it is a day when we give thanks for our many blessings. It is a happy day of family reunions and parties.

A WALNUT SHELL TURKEY

You can make a very lifelike turkey from a piece of cardboard, two walnut shells, and a few feathers. When brightly painted, he makes an out-of-the-ordinary place card and Thanksgiving party favor.

First draw the outline of the head and body on cardboard and cut it out in one piece. Next, glue a walnut shell to each side of the figure, as in the drawing. Whittle wooden legs and glue them to the body. You can use toothpicks, pins or wire for the legs, if you wish. Glue the legs to a small heavy cardboard base. Write your guest's name on the base.

Paint the turkey's beak bright yellow and his head red, and color his body white, red or any other color you like. You don't have to stick to the colors of a real turkey. When the paint is dry, glue a few small feathers to the tail and to the sides of the walnuts. Paint on the eyes or glue small buttons or beads to the head.

CLOTHESPIN PEOPLE

Until you try it, you can scarcely believe how many different kinds of people you can make from clothespins. They are naturally shaped like a human figure, and all that is necessary is to give them faces of different kinds, and dress them, either by painting on the costumes or making skirts, blouses or dresses out of paper or scraps of cloth. Hats are cut from stiff paper or cloth and glued on. If the figure needs arms, twist a piece of pipe cleaner around the top of the body.

Make people like those shown in the drawings. You can make hair for the girls by gluing woolen yarn or embroidery floss to the heads. The figures can be made to stand upright by gluing them to pieces of cardboard.

Place the little figures in the center of the table or on top of a bowl of fruit. They make amusing table decorations.

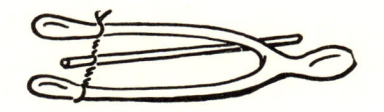

WISHBONE SKIPJACKS

If you get the wishbone on Thanksgiving Day, try making a skipjack with it. Let the wishbone dry out for a day or two. Then take a piece of string, double it, and tie it to the wishbone as shown in the drawing.

Then take a wooden match or other small stick of wood a little shorter than the wishbone, cut a couple of notches in it about ½ inch from one end, and put this end between the double string. Using the match as a lever, twist the string round and round until it is tightly wound up. Then pull the match up toward the head of the wishbone until the string slips into the notches and holds it tight.

To make the skipjack perform, place it on a table with the long end of the match or stick underneath, as in the drawing. The moment you let go of the match, the wishbone will spring into the air, making a leap of several feet.

CHANGING AN ORANGE INTO AN APPLE

This trick is fun to fix up, and the effect is very unexpected and mystifying. An orange, covered by a napkin, is on a plate. When the napkin is lifted, the orange has vanished and an apple has taken its place. Try this trick at your Thanksgiving party.

To prepare the trick, cut an orange into quarters and carefully remove the peel. Fix the four pieces of peel around an apple and at a short distance it will look exactly like an orange. The deception will be more perfect if you cut the orange so as to keep the four quarters joined at the top. This also helps when you secretly remove the peels during the trick.

Put the orange on a plate on your table. Show it to the spectators without lifting it from the plate. Then cover it with a napkin, reach beneath it for a moment to remove the peels, and carry them away as you raise the napkin.

FEEDING THE ELEPHANT

This is a good game for a Thanksgiving Day party. Get an empty, round oatmeal box or any square or oblong box with a top about the same size as an oatmeal box. Put it on a table to be the elephant's mouth.

Then toss peanuts at the box from a throwing line about eight feet away. Each player is given twelve peanuts and throws three at each turn. Each peanut that lands in the elephant's mouth scores one point and, of course, the person with the most points wins.

Date Due — Demco 38-301

DEC 14	FEB 27	NOV 28 1977	AP 6	NO 28 '88
DEC 7	AUG 10 1972	DEC 10 1977	NO 9	JA 30 '89
APR 24	OCT 5 1977	FEB 23 1978		DE 6 '90
JUN 23	DEC 8	MAR 23 1978	MAY 3	
AUG 25	APR 13 1973	NOV 24	NOV 21	
OCT 18	MAR 29 1975	DEC 16 1978	DEC 19	
NOV 8		NO 12 79	MAR 25	
FEB 21	DEC 19 1975	DE -5 '80	DE 29 '86	
DEC 14	NOV 27 1976	DEC 7	SE 8 '87	

DISCARD

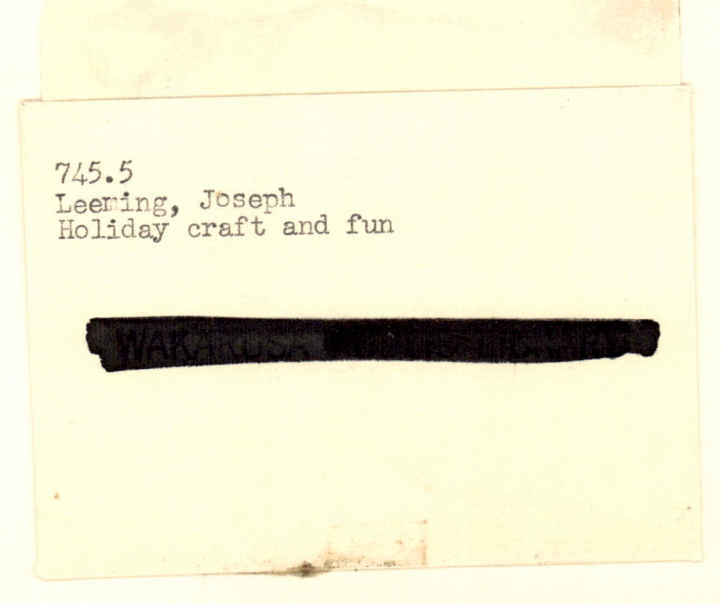

745.5
Leeming, Joseph
Holiday craft and fun